Essays for
COLLEGE & COMPETITIVE EXAMINATIONS

Other Books on
WORD POWER SERIES

1. School Essays, Letters, Applications, and Stories For Higher Secondary Students **(New)** — 110/-
2. Idiomatic English **(New)** — 175/-
3. Effective English Comprehension Read Fast, Understand Better ! **(New)** — 160/-
4. Latest Essays for College & Competitive Examinations **(New)** — 150/-
5. Dictionary of New Words **(New)** — 125/-
6. Art of English Conversation Speak English Fluently **(New)** — 125/-
7. Teach Yourself English Grammar & Composition — 125/-
8. Common & Uncommon Proverbs **(New)** — 125/-
9. Effective Editing Help Yourself in Becoming a Good Editor **(New)** — 150/-
10. Effective English A Boon for Learners **(New)** — 125/-
11. Essays for Primary Classes — 60/-
12. Essays for Junior Classes — 60/-
13. Essays for Senior Classes — 60/-
14. Dictionary of Synonyms and Antonyms — 150/-
15. Dictionary of Idioms and Phrases — 150/-
16. Common Phrases — 125/-
17. How to Write & Speak Correct English — 150/-
18. Meaningful Quotes — 175/-
19. Punctuation Book — 125/-
20. Top School Essays — 110/-
21. How to Write Business Letters with CD — 250/-
22. Everyday Grammar — 150/-
23. Everyday Conversation — 150/-
24. Letters for All Occasions — 125/-
25. School Essays & Letters for Juniors — 110/-
26. Common Mistakes in English — 125/-
27. The Power of Writing — 150/-
28. Learn English in 21 Lessons — 125/-
29. First English Dictionary — 125/-
30. Boost Your Spelling Power — 125/-
31. Self-Help to English Conversation — 125/-
32. The Art of Effective Communication — 125/-
33. A Book of Proverbs & Quotations — 110/-
34. Word Power Made Easy — 160/-
35. English Grammar Easier Way — 160/-
36. General English for Competitive Examinations — 150/-
37. Spoken English — 125/-
38. School Essays, Letters Writing and Phrases — 125/-
39. How to Write & Speak Better English — 125/-
40. Quote Unquote (A Handbook of Famous Quotations) — 160/-
41. Improve Your Vocabulary — 150/-
42. Common Errors in English — 150/-
43. The Art of Effective Letter Writing — 125/-
44. Synonyms & Antonyms — 125/-
45. Idioms — 125/-
46. Business Letters — 125/-

LATEST ESSAYS for

COLLEGE & COMPETITIVE EXAMINATIONS

B.D. Sharma

Lotus PRESS
4735/22, Prakash Deep Building,
Ansari Road, Daryaganj,
New Delhi - 110002

Lotus Press Publishers & Distributors
Unit No.220, 2nd Floor, 4735/22, Prakash Deep Building,
Ansari Road, Daryaganj, New Delhi- 110002
Ph:- 32903912, 23280047, 098118-38000
Email : lotuspress1984@gmail.com
Visit us : www.lotuspress.co.in

Latest Essays for College & Competitive Examinations
© 2016, B.D. Sharma
ISBN : 81-8382-267-1

All rights reserved. No part of this publication may be reproduced, stored in a retrieval system, or transmitted, in any form or by any means, mechanical, photocopying, recording or otherwise, without prior written permission of the publisher.

Printed & Published by : **Lotus Press Publishers & Distributors**, New Delhi- 2

PREFACE

An essay can be defined as "a short literary composition on a single subject, usually presenting the personal view of the author." Essays can consist of a number of elements, including: literary criticism, political manifestos, learned arguments, observations of daily life, recollections, and reflections of the author.

The word essay derives from the French infinitive essayer, "to try" or "to attempt". In English, essay first meant "a trial" or "an attempt", and this is still an alternative meaning. The Frenchman Michel de Montaigne (1533–1592) was the first author to describe his work as essays; he used the term to characterize these as "attempts" to put his thoughts adequately into writing, and his essays grew out of his common-placing.

An essay can have many purposes, but the basic structure is the same no matter what. You may be writing an essay to argue for a particular point of view or to explain the steps necessary to complete a task.

This book is a compilation of several essays on a wide range of topics ranging from economy, society, sports, self-confidence, management, leadership, agriculture, secularism etc. We have tried to cover many recent topics which may be of immense use for the students of different segments and for the students preparing for the competitive exams. We hope that this book will be well appreciated by all the readers.

Author

CONTENTS

1. **Essay: An Introduction** 11
2. **Essays** 24
   Importance of Good First Impression 24

   Change things to Climb Success Ladder 30

   Security on the Internet 34

   Jan Lokpal Bill 40

   Urbanization: A Daunting Challenge 46

   Agriculture and Food Management in India 51

   Globalization in the New Century 56

   Secularism in India 60

   Re-Engineering and Total Quality Management (TQM) 64

   Infrastructure: The Key to Rapid Growth 67

   Rich-Poor Divide: Can It Be Bridged? 72

   Financial Sector Reforms in India 77

   Role of Banks and Financial Institutions in Economy 82

Barack Hussein Obama 87

Reforms in Governance and Poverty Alleviation 93

Self-Communication Solves Personal Problems 98

Importance of Self-Confidence 104

Census 2011 109

Technology—Bane or Boon? 111

Economic Reforms in India 115

Successful Versus Effective Leader 118

The Role of a Manager in an Organization 121

The Tasks of a Leader 123

Management: Its Nature and Scope 126

What is Wrong with Child Labour? 129

Tradition and Modernity: Friends or Foes? 132

Promotion of Sports: A Social Necessity 135

Fast Life: Thrill or Thorn? 139

Prosperity Through Environment 142

Learning from our Failures as well as Success 147

Global Warming 150

India's Urban Scenario 155

How Safe are Mobile Phones? 161

Should Steroids Be Banned? 165

Corruption and Quality of Governance 170

Education for All 176

Widespread Influence of Mahatma Gandhi 181

Inflation in India: Fuelled by Demand? 188

How to Plan your Career? 194

Emergence of New Words, Idioms in the Language 199

The Retailing Scenario in India 205

Rise of Entrepreneurs in India 211

Global Tobacco Epidemic 216

Child Labour 221

Labour Issues in India – Brief Overview 224

India's Foreign Policy: Its Twists and Turns 226

The Telangana Issue 231

Women Empowerment 235

Does TV Reflect Reality? 240

Social Structure in India 246

NSG Waiver and Indo-US Nuclear Deal 252

Indian Democracy and Rule of Law 258

The Issue of Energy Problems 265

Life Saving Drugs– Antibiotics 270

India's Achievements after Independence 273

Telecommuting 277

Retirement at 65? 279

Social Networking Sites: Good or Bad? 281

Reservation 285

Commonwealth Games 290

Black Money 295

Egypt Crisis 297

Aggression in Human Beings 301

State of India's Current Economy 306

Chapter 1

Essay: An Introduction

An essay is usually a short piece of writing which is quite often written from an author's personal point of view. Essays can consist of a number of elements, including: literary criticism, political manifestos, learned arguments, observations of daily life, recollections, and reflections of the author. The definition of an essay is vague, overlapping with those of an article and a short story. Essays have become a major part of a formal education. Secondary students are taught structured essay formats to improve their writing skills, and admission essays are often used by universities in selecting applicants and, in the humanities and social sciences, as a way of assessing the performance of students during final exams. The concept of an "essay" has been extended to other mediums beyond writing.

An essay has been defined in a variety of ways. One definition is a "prose composition with a focused subject of discussion" or a "long, systematic discourse".

It is difficult to define the genre into which essays fall. Aldous Huxley, a leading essayist, gives guidance on the subject. He notes that "Like the novel, the essay is a literary device for saying almost everything about almost anything, usually on a certain topic. By tradition, almost by definition, the essay is a short piece, and it is therefore impossible to give things all full play within the limits of a single essay". He points out that "a collection of essays can cover almost as much ground, and cover it almost as thoroughly, as can a long novel"—he gives Montaigne's Third Book as an example. Huxley argues that "Essays belong to a literary species whose extreme variability can be studied most effectively within a three-poled frame of reference".

Huxley's three poles are:

- *Personal and the autobiographical essays:* These use "fragments of reflective autobiography" to "look at the world through the keyhole of anecdote and description".
- *Objective and factual:* In these essays, the authors "do not speak directly of themselves, but turn their attention outward to some literary or scientific or political theme".
- *Abstract-universal:* These essays "make the best ... of all the three worlds in which it is possible for the essay to exist".

The word essay derives from the French infinitive essayer, "to try" or "to attempt". In English essay first meant "a trial" or "an attempt", and this is still an alternative meaning. The Frenchman Michel de Montaigne (1533–1592) was the first author to describe his work as essays; he used the term to characterize these as "attempts" to put his thoughts adequately into writing, and his essays grew out of his common placing. Inspired in particular by the works of Plutarch, a translation of whose *Oeuvres morales* (Moral works) into French had just been published by Jacques Amyot, Montaigne began to compose his essays in 1572; the first edition, entitled *Essais*, was published in two volumes in 1580. For the rest of his life he continued revising previously published essays and composing new ones. Francis Bacon's essays, published in book form in 1597, 1612, and 1625, were the first works in English that described themselves as essays. Ben Jonson first used the word essayist in English in 1609, according to the Oxford English Dictionary.

"An essay can have many purposes, but the basic structure is the same no matter what. You may be writing an essay to argue for a particular point of view or to explain the steps necessary to complete a task. Either way, your essay will have the same basic format."

If you follow a few simple steps, you will find that the essay almost writes itself. You will be responsible only for supplying ideas, which are the important part of the essay anyway.

These simple steps will guide you through the essay writing process:
- Decide on your topic.
- Prepare an outline or diagram of your ideas.
- Write your thesis statement.
- Write the introduction.
- Write the body.
- Write the main points.
- Write the subpoints.

- Elaborate on the subpoints.
- Add the finishing touches.
- Write the conclusion.

Decide your topic

Topic has been Assigned

You may have no choice as to your topic. If this is the case, you still may not be ready to jump to the next step.

Think about the type of essay you are expected to produce. Should it be a general overview, or a specific analysis of the topic? If it should be an overview, then you are probably ready to move to the next step. If it should be a specific analysis, make sure your topic is fairly specific. If it is too general, you must choose a narrower subtopic to discuss.

For example, the topic "KENYA" is a general one. If your objective is to write an overview, this topic is suitable. If your objective is to write a specific analysis, this topic is too general. You must narrow it to something like "Politics in Kenya" or "Kenya's Culture."

Once you have determined that your topic will be suitable, you can move on.

Topic has not been Assigned

If you have not been assigned a topic, then the whole world lies before you. Sometimes that seems to make the task of starting even more intimidating.

Actually, this means that you are free to choose a topic of interest to you, which will often make your essay a stronger one.

Define your Purpose

The first thing you must do is think about the purpose of the essay you must write. Is your purpose to persuade people to believe as you do, to explain to people how to complete a particular task, to educate people about some person, place, thing or idea, or something else entirely? Whatever topic you choose or have assingned, must fit that purpose.

Brainstorm Subjects of Interest

Once you have determined the purpose of your essay, write down some subjects that interest you. No matter what the purpose of your essay is, an endless number of topics will be suitable.

If you have trouble thinking of subjects, start by looking around you. Is there anything in your surroundings that interests you? Think about your life. What occupies most of your time? That might make for a good topic. Don't evaluate the subjects yet; just write down anything that springs to mind.

Evaluate each Potential Topic

If you can think of at least a few topics that would be appropriate, you must simply consider each one individually. Think about how you feel about that topic. If you want to educate, be sure it is a subject about which you are particularly well-informed. If you want to persuade, be sure it is a subject about which you are at least moderately passionate.

Even if none of the subjects you thought of seem particularly appealing, try just choosing one to work with. It may turn out to be a better topic than at first thought.

Of course, the most important factor in choosing a topic is the number of ideas you have about that topic.

Before you are ready to move on in the essay-writing process, look one more time at the topic you have selected. Think about the type of essay you are expected to produce. Should it be a general overview, or a specific analysis of the topic? If it should be an overview, then you are probably ready to move to the next step. If it should be a specific analysis, make sure your topic is fairly specific. If it is too general, you must choose a narrower subtopic to discuss. Once you have determined that your topic will be suitable, you can move on.

Organize your Ideas

Prepare an outline or diagram of your ideas on paper, in a moderately organized format. The structure you create here may still change before the essay is complete, so don't agonize over this.

Diagram

1. Begin your diagram with a circle or a horizontal line or whatever shape you prefer in the middle of the page.
2. Inside the shape or on the line, write your topic.
3. From your centre shape or line, draw three or four lines out into the page. Be sure to spread them out.
4. At the end of each of these lines, draw another circle or horizontal line or whatever you drew in the centre of the page.
5. In each shape or on each line, write the main ideas that you have about your topic, or the main points that you want to make.

- If you are trying to persuade, you want to write your best arguments.
- If you are trying to explain a process, you want to write the steps that should be followed.

  You will probably need to group these into categories.

  If you have trouble grouping the steps into categories, try using Beginning, Middle, and End.
- If you are trying to inform, you want to write the major categories into which your information can be divided.

6. From each of your main ideas, draw three or four lines out into the page.
7. At the end of each of these lines, draw another circle or horizontal line or whatever you drew in the centre of the page.
8. In each shape or on each line, write the facts or information that support that main idea.

When you have finished, you have the basic structure for your essay and are ready to continue.

Outline

1. Begin your outline by writing your topic at the top of the page.
2. Next, write the Roman numerals I, II, and III, spread apart down the left side of the page.
3. Next to each Roman numeral, write the main ideas that you have about your topic, or the main points that you want to make.
   - If you are trying to persuade, you want to write your best arguments.

- If you are trying to explain a process, you want to write the steps that should be followed.

  You will probably need to group these into categories.

  If you have trouble grouping the steps into categories, try using Beginning, Middle, and End.

- If you are trying to inform, you want to write the major categories into which your information can be divided.

4. Under each Roman numeral, write A, B, and C down the left side of the page.
5. Next to each letter, write the facts or information that support that main idea.

When you have finished, you have the basic structure for your essay and are ready to continue.

Compose a Thesis Statement

Now, that you have decided, at least tentatively, what information you plan to present in your essay, you are ready to formulate your thesis statement.

The thesis statement tells the reader what the essay will be about, and what point you, the author, will be making. You know about your topic.

Now you must look at your outline or diagram and decide what point you will be making. What do the main ideas and supporting ideas that you listed say about your topic?

Your thesis statement will have two parts. The first part states the topic:

- Kenya's Culture

- Building a Model Train Set
- Public Transportation

The second part states the point of the essay:

- has a rich and varied history
- takes time and patience
- can solve some of our city's most persistent and pressing problems

    Or in the second part you could simply list the three main ideas you will discuss.

- has a long history, blends traditions from several other cultures, and provides a rich heritage.
- requires an investment in time, patience, and materials.
- helps with traffic congestion, resource management, and the city budget.

Once you have formulated a thesis statement that fits this pattern and with which you are comfortable, you are ready to continue.

Write the Body Paragraphs

In the body of the essay, all the preparation up to this point comes to fruition. The topic you have chosen must now be explained, described, or argued.

Each main idea that you wrote down in your diagram or outline will become one of the body paragraphs. If you had three or four main ideas, you will have three or four body paragraphs.

Each body paragraph will have the same basic structure.

1. Start by writing down one of your main ideas, in

sentence form. If your main idea is "reduces freeway congestion," you might say this: Public transportation reduces freeway congestion.
2. Next, write down each of your supporting points for that main idea, but leave four or five lines in between each point.
3. In the space under each point, write down some elaboration for that point. *Elaboration* can further be description or explanation or discussion.

Supporting Point

Commuters appreciate the cost savings of taking public transportation rather than driving.

Elaboration

Less driving time means less maintenance expense, such as oil changes. Of course, less driving time means savings on gasoline as well. In many cases, these savings amount to more than the cost of riding public transportation.

4. If you wish, include a summary sentence for each paragraph.

   This is not generally needed, however, and such sentences have a tendency to sound stilted, so be cautious about using them.

Once you have fleshed out of each of your body paragraphs, one for each main point, you are ready to continue.

Write the Introduction and Conclusion

Your essay lacks only two paragraphs now: the introduction and the conclusion. These paragraphs will give the reader a point of entry to and a point of exit from your essay.

Introduction

The introduction should be designed to attract the reader's attention and give her an idea of the essay's focus.

1. Begin with an attention grabber.

The attention grabber you use is up to you, but here are some ideas:

- Starting Information

    This information must be true and verifiable, and it doesn't need to be totally new to your readers. It could simply be a pertinent fact that explicitly illustrates the point you wish to make.

    If you use a piece of starting information, follow it with a sentence or two of elaboration.

- Anecdote

    An *anecdote* is a story that illustrates a point.

    Be sure your anecdote is short, to the point, and relevant to your topic. This can be a very effective opener for your essay, but use it carefully.

- Dialogue

    An appropriate dialogue does not have to identify the speakers, but the reader must understand the point you are trying to convey. Use only two or three exchanges between speakers to make your point. Follow dialogue with a sentence or two of elaboration.

- Summary Information

    Few sentences explaining your topic in general terms can lead the reader gently to your thesis. Each sentence should become gradually more specific, until you reach your thesis.

2. If the attention grabber was only a sentence or two, add one or two more sentences that will lead the reader from your opening to your thesis statement.
3. Finish the paragraph with your thesis statement.

Conclusion

The conclusion brings closure to the reader, summing up your points or providing a final perspective on your topic.

All the conclusions need three or four strong sentences which do not need to follow any set formula. Simply review the main points (being careful not to restate them exactly) or briefly describe your feelings about the topic. Even an anecdote can end your essay in a useful way.

Add the Finishing Touches

You have now completed all of the paragraphs of your essay. Before you can consider this a finished product, however, you must give some thought to the formatting of your essay.

Check the order of your Paragraphs

Look at your paragraphs. Which one is the strongest? You might want to start with the strongest paragraph, end with the second strongest, and put the weakest in the middle. Whatever order you decide on, be sure it makes sense. If your essay is describing a process, you will probably need to stick to the order in which the steps must be completed.

Check the Instructions for the Assignment

When you prepare a final draft, you must be sure to follow all of the instructions you have been given.

- Are your margins correct?
- Have you titled it as directed?
- What other information (name, date, etc.) must you include?
- Did you double-space your lines?

Check your Writing

Nothing can substitute for revision of your work. By reviewing what you have done, you can improve weak points that otherwise would be missed. Read and reread your paper.

- Does it make logical sense?

    Leave it for a few hours and then read it again. Does it still make logical sense?

- Do the sentences flow smoothly from one another?

    If not, try to add some words and phrases to help connect them. Transition words, such as "therefore" or "however," sometimes help. Also, you might refer in one sentence to a thought in the previous sentence. This is especially useful when you move from one paragraph to another.

- Have you run a spell checker or a grammar checker?

    These aids cannot catch every error, but they might some catch errors that you have missed.

■ ■ ■

CHAPTER 2

Essays

Importance of Good First Impression

First impression is the last impression. Thus goes a well-known platitude. Many, doubting the veracity of the statement ignore its importance affect and face difficulties in life. Others harm or damage their chances of success in interviews.

They are cocky about their merit. Hence, they think that they ignore the wisdom in this saying. In any case, making a first good impression is a sure personality asset, not a liability. Therefore, it must be put high on the list of personality plus points.

There are reasons for it. Man is a social animal. We have to interact with people. The impression we create and leave on people trails us. We cannot escape from it. Our attitude to other people is more important than attitude to us. People take us as they find us. If we are friendly and outward looking, interested and zestful, people like us and accept us. If we lack these qualities, they tend to distance themselves from us. Positive approach makes easy for us to get along with others. Also, we leave a nice impression.

This has other advantages, too. We create social opportunities for ourselves by going out, meeting and building bridges. Sharing activities forges chains of friendship.

It is we, ourselves, who put strain on human relations. A foul-mouthed man, however attractive in his physical appearance, is bound to leave a bad impression. One who speaks a pleasant word obviously leaves behind a pleasant impression.

There is no need to be theatrical or over-dramatic. You are not a film star. In order to create a good impression, it's necessary to be natural and at an ease. Let others see and meet the real you!

There is no denying the vital fact that, at heart, we want recognition, acceptance and appreciation. We cannot isolate ourselves totally from others and lead a full and satisfying life. When we cut ourselves from others, we become an island of isolation.

However, this does not mean that we should become crawling cowards. Each and every action of ours should be calculated to please others.

When it is a question of self-respect or conviction, we should act differently. That is rightly whatever others may think.

Yet, a major portion of our life is linked with the life of others. This cannot be ignored. This naturally concerns what they think of us and what they expect of us.

Ladder of Success. The inference is: the youngster striving to go up the ladder of success in life must do all he can to make a good impression on others. That's one way he gets their nod.

The impression that we first create on others may or may not matter but it counts. Opinions in the light of experiences may change, but the first impression does stick.

Thus, it is important to cultivate it. It is better to present a surface which cannot be challenged, rather than a surface which has to undergo a drastic change later, or at one stage after another. The surface must be genuine.

If it is a fake, it will be seen through. No one can put on an act for all times. No one can fool all the people, all the time.

It implies that we have to be natural otherwise the impression is blighted. This means that our real self must be winsome. This is what we must work on. Not the fake impression, which can be faulted.

Thus, we should strive for a face-lift of personality so that it has a winsome and magnetic influence on people we rub shoulders with.

We should strive to build a sort of personality which

makes up an instant and pleasant impact on those we come in contact with.

The first impression we make on others is of great consequence. Sometimes, we do have to revise our impression. Even then the importance of the first impression does not lose its validity totally.

Many youngsters nurse the notion that they can act smart; that they can put on a show and get away with it. One may say: "Today, I am meeting so-and-so. I will pull a fast one on him. How can he ever know it?" He may succeed but he is likely to get into an act-pattern, which will eventually show him in poor light. Society holds and shows him the mirror!

What are the factors that go in making a pleasant and winsome impression? We pinpoint some. In this list, the reader is free to add his own recipes, if any.

Appearance. A strikingly well-dressed woman or man has an edge over others; at least so far as physical appearance is concerned.

Now, think of the opposite and draw your own conclusion.

Not many have this edge because God has not bestowed on them the attributes of attractive physical appearance. But it is all the more reasons that we should strive to create an impact we can. This means extra care on neatness, grooming, cleanliness and posture that speak loud in our favour.

Assets should not be concealed. They should be

revealed. They should be highlighted. This shows self-respect. We cannot expect others to respect us if we count down our own selves.

Generate your own steam. It is one of the biggest assets we often ignore at much cost. Pleasant speech is the hallmark of a winsome personality as it makes a nice impression. Otherwise people say, "He is nice so long as he does not open his mouth." A grating screeching voice spoils impression. Cultivation of voice pays dividends.

Charming people usually have a friendly and cheerful voice. They convey amiability and warmth. Those who have seen Raj Kapoor's movies will concede that he had a magnetic voice, which contributed a lot to his charisma.

Words link us to others. They are useful instruments. They work both ways: they can create pleasantness, and also cause offence. Sarcastic words, couched in acidic tones, go a long way in creating enemies. A colleague known for his foul-mouth was nicknamed "cobra" for he was always hissing with his words!

Words and their meanings similarly matter a lot. Quite often we take words and their meanings for granted. A friend introducing me to a relative of his said: "Mr Soni is an upstart in writing." What he meant was that I was upcoming as a writer.

The tone too is important. A rasping, harsh tone dispels others. A whining one creates gloom. A cheerful chuckle comes out as if pearls are falling out of a jar.

Genuine. Pretension of superiority or authority also repels people as no one likes to be made inferior. The bossy ones are usually disliked, if not hated. The pompous ones become laughable. If you are laughed at, you are making a scene not an impression.

In short, cultivate the art of speaking in tones calculated to attract rather than repel. Positives attract. Negatives repel. For example: courtesy attracts; curtness repels.

Similarly, bad and misfit words and vocabulary go a long way in creating a question mark against personality.

Pay a compliment. Don't be niggardly in doing so. There is a good way to compensate for this lack: listen attentively to the person who is talking to you. He will be impressed. Listening attentively is also a compliment. Refusal to compliment amounts to criticism.

Change things to Climb Success Ladder

Why modern organizations have a hard time transforming themselves is that leaders are having a difficult time transforming themselves.

Unfortunately, after many years of work they begin to believe in their own infallibility. After all, they are the experts.

In such a mindset, they forget that the expert of today is the giant of tomorrow. To become successful leaders today, who will continue to be successful tomorrow, we must become beginners!

Habitual thinking tends to get in the way when we want to create new ideas. Many of us want to run off the edge of a cliff. How do you deal with a habit not productive for you; a habit that's not working for you?

The best way to deal with such a habit is to replace it with a habit that is working for you. So the next time you have a tough problem to solve, consider some creativity habits.

Ask Yourself

"How else can I do this?" Socrates says "When you always do what you do, you always get now."?But if you want to make some changes in what is going on in your organization, that's good reason to begin using some now creativity habits.

By the way, if the Socrates phrase doesn't work for you, try this one: Insanity is doing the same thing over and over while expecting different results."

French writer Voltaire, once said, "Judge a person by his questions rather than his answers."

Adopt ways to get new ideas that come "free". Leaders get their good ideas while driving, taking a shower or as they do nothing!

Catch those ideas when they appear. Keep a piece of paper, a note pad to packet the new insights. A friend of mine uses his voice recorder to store his new ideas so he can listen to them. Use whatever method works for you.

When you are on a vacation you change your routine. You are not in familiar surroundings. Dr. Gerard Puccio says, there is a direct relationship between the distance he is away from home and the numbers of new ideas he generates. For Gerard, the farther away from home, the more ideas he creates!

Vacation

Instead of thinking about what is going to happen at office, focus on the world around you. Take a mini-vacation on the way to work! Try a different way or get off the expressway and take the scenic route by exposing yourself to some different scenery and you are likely to get some new input. Look out of the window instead of burying your nose in the morning paper.

One study found that "slugs" read almost nothing, the "productive" read almost exclusively in their field, while the "innovative" read in a variety of fields. In fact, a great deal of people read everything, from science fiction to technical journals, from popular mechanics to psychology, and therefore enjoy a much richer storehouse. Thus, they generate more new ideas.

A teacher in a food service organization tells young graduates "If you want to find out what is going on in the food service industry today, read Institutional Management or Restaurant News. But if you want to find out what is going to in this field in the future, read Psychology Today."

To spot the trends of the future and to get new information you need to read outside of your area.

Interaction

It is important to interact with people from varying backgrounds who have a variety of interests. This may not be easy, for we find it more comfortable to spend time with people familiar to us.

The best source of new information is not from the people you see regularly. They usually have the same information as you have. The best source of new information is from other networks—people who run in circles different from your own.

To spur your creativity, it is important to tap into groups of people with whom you usually don't interact. Find those new networks and plug into them.

It is crucial to have personal and professional relationship that can provide you with a support system when the going gets tough.

Environment that Encourages Creativity

Have you ever walked into a place, rubbed your hands together, and said to yourself, "I could really do some great work here?"

Artists and musicians have studios, craftsmen have workshops, professors have studies, and scientists have laboratories. Where is your creative space? Where do you go to do your best work?

The extreme case was the philosopher Kant, who would work in bed at certain times of the day with the blankets arranged around him in a specific fashion—while writing Kant would concentrate on a tower visible from his window.

When some trees grew up to hide the tower, he became frustrated and the city fathers cut down the trees so that he could continue his work!

Now, we are not advocating that you stock your desk with decaying fruit or cut the trees in your neighbourhood. But think about it for a minute; what are the attributes of your optimal working environment?

Do you do your best work with music playing or in silence? Are you a morning person or an evening person? Is you space filled with light, or is it dim? Is it cool or warm?

Do you sip coffees or snack while you work? Is your ideal work environment formal or informal? Do you have desks and tables neatly arranged in your space, or is your area informal with pillows and cushions scattered about the place?

What is your preferred working environment? What environment helps you become the most comfortable and productive?

When you begin to more closely examine your working style preferences and change your environment to support your preferences, you will not only increase your creativity, but also will increase your productivity as well.

■ ■ ■

Security on the Internet

How do you secure something that is changing faster than you can fix it? The Internet has had security problems since its earliest days as a pure research project.

Today, after several years and orders of magnitude of growth, is still has security problems. It is being used for a purpose for which it was never intended: commerce.

It is somewhat ironic that the early Internet was design as a prototype for a high-availability command and control network that could resist outages resulting from enemy actions, yet it cannot resist college undergraduates. The problem is that the attackers are on, and make up apart of, the network they are attacking.

Designing a system that is capable of resisting attack from within, while still growing and evolving at a breakneck pace, is probably impossible. Deep infrastructure changes are needed, and once you have achieved a certain amount of size, the sheer inertia of the installed base may make it impossible to apply fixes.

While some technologies have been developed, only an industry-wide effort and cooperation can minimize risks and ensure privacy for users, data confidentiality for the financial institutions, and nonrepudiation for electronic commerce.

The World Wide Web is the single largest, most ubiquitous source of information in the world, and it sprang up spontaneously.

People use interactive Web pages to obtain stock quotes,

receive tax information from the Internal Revenue Service, make appointments with a hairdresser, consult a pregnancy planner to determine ovulation dates, conduct election polls, register for a conference, search for old friends, and the list goes on.

It is only natural that the Web's functionality, popularity, and ubiquity have made it the seemingly ideal platform for conducting electronic commerce. People can now go online to buy CDs, clothing, concert tickets, and stocks.

Several companies, such Digicash, Cybercash, and First Virtual, have sprung up to provide mechanisms for conducting business on the Web. The savings in cost and the convenience of shopping via the Web are incalculable.

Whereas most successful computer systems result from careful, methodical planning, followed by hard work, the Web took on a life of its own from the very beginning.

The introduction of a common protocol and a friendly graphical user interface was all that was needed to ignite the Internet explosion.

The Web's virtues are extolled without end, but its rapid growth and universal adoption have not been without cost. In particular, security was added as an afterthought.

New capabilities were added ad hoc to satisfy the growing demand for features without carefully considering the impact on security.

As general-purpose scripts were introduced on both the client and the server sides, the dangers of accidental and malicious abuse grew. It did not take long for the Web to move from the scientific community to the commercial world. At this point, the security threats became much more serious.

The incentive for malicious attackers to exploit vulnerabilities in the underlying technologies is at an all-time high. This is indeed frightening when we consider what attackers of computer systems have accomplished when their only incentive was fun and boosting their egos.

When business and profit are at stake, we cannot assume anything less than the most dedicated and resourceful attackers typing their utmost to steal, cheat, and perform malice against users of the Web.

There are simple and advanced methods for ensuring browser security and protecting user privacy. The more simple techniques are user certification schemes, which rely on digital Ids.

Netscape Communicator Navigator and Internet Explorer allow users to obtain and use personal certificates.

Currently, the only company offering such certificates is Verisign, which offers digital Ids that consist of a certificate of a user's identity, signed by Verisign.

There are four classes of digital Ids, each represents a different level of assurance in the identify, and each comes at an increasingly higher cost. The assurance is determined by the effort that goes into identifying the person requesting the certificate.

Many Web sites require their users to register a name and a password. When users connect to these sites, their browser pops up an authentication window that asks for these two items.

Usually, the browser than sends the name and password to the server that can allow retrieval of the remaining pages at the site. The authentication information can be protected from eavesdropping and replay by using the SSL protocol.

Today, firewalls are sold by many vendors and protect tens of thousands of sites. The products are a far cry from the first-generation firewalls, now including fancy graphical user interfaces, intrusion detection systems, and various forms of tamper-proof software.

To operate, a firewall sits between the protected network and all external access points. To work effectively, firewalls have to guard all access points into the network's perimeter otherwise, an attacker can simply go around the firewall and attack an undefended connection.

The simple days of the firewalls ended when the Web exploded. Suddenly, instead of handling only a few simple services in an "us versus them manner", firewalls now must be connected with complex data and protocols.

Today's firewall has to handle multimedia traffic level, attached downloadable programs (applets) and a host of other protocols plugged into Web browsers.

This development has produced a basis conflict: The firewall is in the way of the things users want to do. A second problem has arisen as many sites want to host Web servers.

Does the Web server go inside or outside of the firewall? Firewalls are both a blessing and a curse. Presumably, they help deflect attacks. They also complicate users' lives, make Web server administrators' jobs harder, rob network performance, add an extra point of failure, cost money, and make networks more complex to manage.

Proxy firewalls have evolved to the point where today they support a wide range of services and run on a number of different UNIX and Windows NT platforms.

Many security experts believe that proxy firewall is more secure than other types of firewalls, largely because the first proxy firewalls were able to apply additional control on to the data traversing the proxy. The real reason for proxy firewalls was their ease of implementation, not their security properties.

For security, it does not really matter where in the processing of data the security check is made; what's more important is that it is made at all.

Because they do not allow any direct communication between the protected network and outside world, proxy firewall inherently provide network address translation.

Whenever an outside site gets a connection from the firewall's proxy address, it in turn hides and translates the addresses of system behind the firewall.

Cryptography is at the heart of computer and network security. The important cryptographic functions are encryption, decryption, one-way hashing, and digital signatures.

Ciphers are divided into two categories, symmetric

and asymmetric, or public-key systems. Symmetric ciphers are functions where the same key is used for encryption and decryption.

Public-key systems can be used for encryption, but they are also useful for key agreement and digital signatures. Key-agreement protocols enable two parties to compute a secret key, even in the face of an eavesdropper.

Despite its size and rapid growth, the Web is still in its infancy. So is the software industry. We are just beginning to learn how to develop secure software, and we are beginning to understand that for our future, if it is to be online, we need to incorporate security into the basic underpinnings of everything we develop.

■ ■ ■

Jan Lokpal Bill

In the recent times, the Lokpal Bill has attracted attention of the politicians as well as commoners. The word 'Lokpal' means an ombudsman or Legal Representative in India. The word has been derived from the Sanskrit words 'loka' meaning people and 'pala' meaning protector or caretaker. So, the word Lokpal means 'protector of people'. The concept of Lokpal has been drawn up to root out corruption at all levels in the prevailing Indian polity.

In a nutshell, the Lokpal Bill is a proposed anti-corruption law designed to effectively deter corruption, redress grievances and protect whistleblowers. The law would create an ombudsman called the Lokpal; this would be an independent body similar to the Election Commission of India with the power to prosecute politicians and bureaucrats without prior government permission.

The first Jan Lokpal Bill was introduced by Shanti Bhushan in 1968. It was passed in the 4th Lok Sabha in 1969 but could not get through in the Rajya Sabha. Subsequently, Lokpal bills were introduced in 1971, 1977, 1985, 1989, 1996, 1998, 2001, 2005 and in 2008, yet they were never passed. Unfortunately, even after 42 years of its first introduction, the bill is still pending in India.

For 42 years, the government-drafted bill has failed to pass the Rajya Sabha, the upper house of the Parliament of India.

Following the four day Anna Hazare fasting struggle, Prime Minister Manmohan Singh stated that the Lokpal Bill would be introduced in the 2011 Monsoon Session of Parliament.

Renewed calls for a Jan Lokpal Bill arose over resentment of the major differences between the draft 2010 Lokpal Bill prepared by the government and the Jan Lokpal Bill prepared by the members of this movement, N. Santosh Hegde, a former justice of the Supreme Court of India and Lokayukta of Karnataka, Shanti Bhushan, Arvind Kejriwal and Prashant Bhushan, a senior lawyer in the Supreme Court along with the members of the India Against Corruption movement. The bill's backers consider existing laws too weak and insufficiently enforced to stop corruption.

Key Features of Proposed Bill

Here are some key features of the proposed bill:

- To establish a central government anti-corruption institution called Lokpal, supported by Lokayukta at the state level.
- As in the case of the Supreme Court and Cabinet Secretariat, the Lokpal will be supervised by the Cabinet Secretary and the Election Commission. As a result, it will be completely independent of the government and free from ministerial influence in its investigations.
- Members will be appointed by judges, Indian Administrative Service officers with a clean record,

private citizens and constitutional authorities through a transparent and participatory process.

- A selection committee will invite shortlisted candidates for interviews, videorecordings of which will thereafter be made public.
- Every month on its website, the Lokayukta will publish a list of cases dealt with, brief details of each, their outcome and any action taken or proposed. It will also publish lists of all cases received by the Lokayukta during the previous month, cases dealt with and those which are pending.
- Investigations of each case must be completed in one year. Any resulting trials should be concluded in the following year, giving a total maximum process time of two years.
- Losses caused to the government by a corrupt individual will be recovered at the time of conviction.
- Government office work required by a citizen that is not completed within a prescribed time period will result in Lokpal imposing financial penalties on those responsible, which will then be given as compensation to the complainant.
- Complaints against any officer of Lokpal will be investigated and completed within a month and, if found to be substantive, will result in the officer being dismissed within two months.
- The existing anti-corruption agencies (CVC, departmental vigilance and the anti-corruption branch of the CBI) will be merged into Lokpal which will

have complete power and authority to independently investigate and prosecute any officer, judge or politician.

- Whistleblowers who alert the agency to potential corruption cases will also be provided with protection by it.

On March 13, 2011, a group of Delhi residents dressed in white shirts and t-shirts drove around the city for four hours in support of an anti-corruption campaign and the passing of a Jan Lokpal Bill.

Further, anti-corruption activist Anna Hazare went on hunger strike 'unto death' on April 5, 2011, pending the enactment of a Jan Lokpal Bill. Around 6,000 Mumbai residents also began a one-day fast in support of similar demands. The protests were not associated with any political parties, and Hazare supporters discouraged political leaders from joining the protests, because Hazare believes that political parties were using the campaign for their own political advantage.

To dissuade Hazare from going on an indefinite hunger strike, the Prime Minister's office have directed the ministries of personnel and law to examine how the views of society activists can be included in the Lokpal Bill.

On 5 April 2011, the National Advisory Council rejected the Lokpal Bill drafted by the government. Union Human Resource Development Minister Kapil Sibal then met social activists Swami Agnivesh and Arvind Kejriwal to find ways to bridge differences over the bill.

Hazare's fast was supported by the CPI(M) with their

politburo issuing a statement demanding an effective Lokpal Bill.

After several rounds of talks, on 8 April 2011, Anna Hazare announced to his supporters that the Government had agreed to all his demands and he would break his fast on the following Saturday morning. According to the understanding reached, five of the ten-member joint-draft committee would come from society. Pranab Mukherjee will be the Chairman of the draft committee and Shanti Bhushan his Co-Chairman.

Government's handling of the formation of the draft committee, involving the civil society in preparation of the draft Lokpal Bill, was criticized by various political parties, including BJP, BJD, AIADMK, CPI-M, RJD, BJD, JD(U) and Samajwadi Party.

The drafting committee was officially formed on 8 April 2011. It consists of ten members, including five from the government and five drawn from society. The Government of India accepted that the committee be co-chaired by a politician and an activist, non-politician. It is reported that Pranab Mukherjee, from the political arena, and Shanti Bhushan, from civil society, will fill those roles.

Some people have opined that the Jan Lokpal Bill is 'Naïve' in its approach to combating corruption. According to Pratap Bhanu Mehta, President, Centre for Policy Research, Delhi, the Bill 'is premised on an institutional imagination that is at best naïve; at worst subversive of representative democracy'. The Lokpal concept was criticized by the Human Resource Development (HRD) minister Kapil Sibal because of concerns that it will lack accountability, oppressively, and undemocratically.

The claim that the Lokpal will be an extra-constitutional body has been derided by Hazare's closest lieutenant, Arvind Kejriwal. He states the Jan Lokpal Bill drafted by civil society will only investigate corruption offences and submit a charge sheet which would then be tried and prosecuted, through trial courts and higher courts. Kejriwal further states that the proposed Bill also lists clear provisions in which the Supreme Court can abolish the Lokpal.

Whatever be the status of the Bill on paper, India is still struggling to rid itself of corruption and shady politicians.

■ ■ ■

Urbanization: A Daunting Challenge

Urbanization has been a problem in India from quite sometime and the local agencies at the state governments in the country have always struggled to solve the problems like growth of slums, management of solid waste, water supply, street lighting, locating the street vendors etc. With the cities contributing more than 65 per cent of the GDP in the recent years, the government has now begun to look at the urban areas as engines of growth. With rapidly increasing population in the urban areas and insurmountable problems, urbanization has emerged as one of the most serious challenges before the planners.

Migration to cities is considered to be a serious problem and most of the political parties as well as the municipal bodies are generally interested in reversing this trend of rapid urbanization.

But migration is not the only reason for growth of the cities. Internal growth of cities and inclusion of the periphery areas are two other reasons for growth of the urban areas. It is expected that in the coming two decades, the urban population share in the total population of the country would increase to 50 per cent.

Rural poor come to the cities and towns to look for productive work with a view to get two square meals for their families and secure better education for their children.

They also migrate to the cities to ensure that they are able to lead a better life than their forefathers and the cities act as the dream destinations for the poor for a better tomorrow. But their dreams get shattered as they

Urbanization: A Daunting Challenge

arrive in the cities. They are hassled by the problems like lack of affordable housing, lack of availability of clean drinking water, lack of cleanliness, sanitation and other civic amenities.

The question is—can we envisage the transformation of the modern day cities in the country without appreciating the contribution of the poorer sections in the overall growth of cities? They render the required and important services like household assistance, street sweeping, solid waste disposal, delivery of newspapers, delivery of milk and other food articles and vegetables etc. But, this important segment of urban population cannot get land security for their dwellings and are generally bereft of even bare minimum urban services in the vicinity of localities where they live.

There is thus a dire need for having the provision of housing for the urban poor. While the cities and towns keep coming out with various housing projects for the upper and middle classes, housing schemes for the urban poor and the low income groups generally do not exist.

But, the poor are required to be uprooted from their slums whenever a new scheme of infrastructure or housing is planned in any city. This trend to be changed.

Lack of civic amenities is yet another problem. As per a slum census, only 65.4 per cent of the households in the cities and towns have an access to drinking water within their premises. Remaining households either have the water supply source outside their premises or away from their houses.

Source of lighting is an another important area which was surveyed during the census. Though the percentage of households having an electric source of energy is much higher in the urban area than in the rural areas, yet more than 12 per cent of the households in the urban areas do not have an electric source of lighting and have to depend on other sources like kerosene. About 0.4 per cent of the households in cities and towns have no source of lighting at all.

Availability of education facilities in the urban areas is also a key area, particularly for the poor. While the affluent and upper middle classes normally have best of educational facilities available to them in the cities, the poorer sections find it hard to have access even to basic educational facilities. The level of male and female literacy rates in the slum areas is distinctly lower than that in non-slum population of cities, with Patna recording highest difference of almost 30 per cent.

Lack of good healthcare facilities is also an area of serious concern. The Task Force appointed by the Government of India to advise on health scenario in the urban slums has pointed out that 6 out of 10 children in slum areas are delivered at home in Indian slums. Further, more than half of India's urban poor children are underweight and the state of under-nutrition in urban areas is worse than in the rural areas. Reach and utilisation of essential preventive health services by the urban poor is generally found to be very low and about 60 per cent of the children below one year of age are not fully immunized. Only 4 per cent couples use birth spacing methods.

In addition to the above mentioned problems pertaining to urban and social services, there are serious gaps in the availability of infrastructure facilities in urban areas. Roads are getting congested with more and more new vehicles getting registered every day and parking has become a serious problem in most urban areas. Solid waste management is also a serious problem in the cities. Safe disposal of the solid waste in a scientific manner is a major issue in Indian cities and towns. With over 400 million people living in urban areas and generating millions of tonnes of garbage every day, without proper arrangements for safe disposal of the garbage serious problems of water contamination and environment pollution are on the anvil. The problem is worst in the areas inhabited by the poor in the slums.

The Road Ahead

From the last about six decades, the government has focused on rural development and rural poverty alleviation. Billions of rupees have been spent, but even after 60 years of concentration on this sector, the absolute number of rural poor in the country has actually increased. The government is now viewing the urbanisation process as an alternative strategy to eradicate rural poverty. Growth rate of population in the cities of the country is much higher than the general growth rate of population in the country and there is a need to strengthen the cities and towns to be able to brace up to the challenges ahead.

The Government of India, in December, 2005, launched an ambitious programme called Jawaharlal Nehru National Urban Renewal Mission (JNNURM), for the renewal of Indian cities on sustainable basis. 63 cities have been chosen under the programme.

There are also two sub-programmes. First sub-programme aims at strengthening the urban infrastructure like water supply, sewerage, traffic flow, de-congestion, scientific solid waste management, proper storm water drainage, preservation of heritage etc. Second sub-programme is aimed at providing basic services to the urban poor, including proper housing at affordable rates and up-gradation of slums to ensure that all the slum areas in that cities are provided with the same level of facilities as are available to the better areas in the other cities.

Funding pattern under the JNNURM is that for the States of the north- east, 90 per cent of the cost of projects approved under the mission is to be provided by the Union Government as grant-in-aid and the remaining amount has to be pooled in by the Urban Local Body (ULB) concerned and the State Government. For other hill States and the cities with less than one million population, the percentage of ACA is 80 per cent. For cities with population between one million and four million, the ACA is 50 per cent of the project cost, while the same for the cities with over four million population is 35 per cent.

It is expected that after including the State and ULB share, during the programme period (upto 2012-13), more than Rs 1,50,000 crore would be spent for up-gradation of urban infrastructure and for providing basic services for urban poor in that cities.

In addition to the JNNURM funding and projects, the city administration has to make special efforts to make sure that the challenges of urbanisation are met and the cities and towns are able to cope up with the urban problems in the coming years.

■■■

Agriculture and Food Management in India

The performance of the agricultural sector influences the growth of the Indian Economy. Agriculture (including allied activities) accounted for 17.8 per cent of the Gross Domestic Product in 2007-08, as compared to 21.7 per cent in 2003-04 at constant price.

Notwithstanding the fact that the share of this sector in GDP has been declining over the years, its role remains critical as it accounts for about 52 per cent of the employment in the country. Apart from being the provider of food and fodder, its importance also stems from the raw materials that it provides to industry. The prosperity of the rural economy is also closely linked to agriculture and allied activities. The rural sector (including agriculture) is being increasingly seen as a potential source of domestic demand; a recognition, that is shaping the marketing strategies of entrepreneurs wishing to widen the demand for goods and services.

Area, Production and Yield

Growth in the production of agricultural crops depends on acreage and yield. Limitations in the expansion of agricultural land suggest that increase in gross cropped area can come from multiple cropping. In view of this, the main source of long-term output growth is improvement in yield.

Compound growth rates of indices of an area under rice showed a negative growth of (-) 0.1 per cent per annum during 2001-08, compared to the 1990s. Area under rice cultivation has remained more or less stagnant in the recent years while growth in yield has shown an increase.

Area under wheat, that was around 25 million hectares in 2002-03, increased to 26.4 million hectares in 2005-06 and further to 28 million hectares in 2007-08. The coverage under irrigation has been about 87 to 89 per cent of area for wheat. The compound growth rates of indices of an area, production and yield of wheat during 1991-2000 and 2001-08 show a perceptible decline.

During 2008-09 the area sown at all-India level under kharif was 2.3 per cent less than the area sown in 2007-08 of 1,039.23 lakh hectares. As on March 27, 2009, area sown under all rabi crops taken together had been reported to be higher at 638.33 lakh hectares, as compared to 619.68 lakh hectares in the corresponding period of 2007-08.

Agricultural Inputs

Improvement in yield, which is a key to long-term growth, depends on a host of factors that include technology, use of quality seeds, fertilizers and pesticides and micro-nutrients, and, not the least, irrigation. Each of these plays a role in determining the yield level and in turn the augmentation in the level of production.

The first decisive step that a farmer takes relates to sowing. The availability of quality seeds (among other factors) makes a critical difference to its output growth. In India, more than four-fifths of farmers rely on farm-saved seeds, leading to a low seed replacement rate.

Irrigation

The Government of India has taken up irrigation potential

creation through public funding and assisting farmers to create potential on their own farms. Substantial irrigation potential has been created through major and medium irrigation schemes. The total irrigation potential in the country had increased from 81.1 million hectares in 1991-92 to 102.08 million hectares up to the end of the Tenth Five Year Plan (2006-07). Of the total potential created, however, only 87.2 million hectares has been actually utilized. The Working Group on Water Resources for the Eleventh Five Year Plan (2007-12) has proposed creation of irrigation potential of 16 million hectares (9 million hectares from MMI sector and 7 million hectares from MI sector) during the Eleventh Five Year Plan period.

Fertilizers

Chemical fertilizers have played a significant role in the development of the agricultural sector. The per hectare consumption of fertilizers in nutrient terms stood at 117.07 kg in 2007-08. However, recent trends in agricultural productivity show a decline in marginal productivity of soil in relation to the application of fertilizers and in some cases, has also become negative. Lack of the application of proper nutrients based on soil analysis has also contributed to slowdown in growth of productivity.

The domestic production of urea in the year 2008-09 was 199.22 lakh tonnes, as compared to 187.27 lakh tonnes in 2002-03.

The government has taken various policy initiatives for the fertilizer sector. These cover pricing policy for indigenous urea, new investments in urea sector, nutrient-based pricing, production and availability of fortified and coated fertilizers, uniform freight subsidy on all fertilizers under the fertilizer subsidy regime, concession scheme for decontrolled phosphatic and potassic fertilizers, inclusion of Mono Ammonium Phosphate (MAP), Tri Super Phosphate (TSP) and Ammonium Sulphate (AS) in the concession scheme, revised scheme for concession for Single Super Phosphate (SSP) based on inputs cost and a uniform all-India maximum retail price of Rs. 3,400 per tonne for SSP, policy for conversion of FO/LSHS urea units to natural gas.

Agriculture Insurance

The frequency and severity of droughts, floods and cyclones, and rising temperatures, agro-climatic variations and erratic rainfall accentuate uncertainty and risk in the agricultural sector leading to huge losses in agricultural production and the livestock population in India.

The National Agriculture Insurance Scheme (NAIS) for crops had been implemented on rabi in 1999-2000 season.

Under the Weather Based Crop Insurance Scheme (WBCIS) being implemented by the Agriculture Insurance Company of India Ltd. (AICIL), 10 States had been covered on pilot basis during the kharif 2008 season. About 1.4 lakh farmers with 1.87 lakh hectares of cropped area were insured for a sum of Rs. 309 crore generating a premium of Rs. 31.5 crore (including subsidy, farmers' share of premium is Rs. 11.82 crore). This pilot is being continued on rabi during 2008-09.

Food Management

Food management in India has three basic objectives *viz.* procurement of food-grains from farmers at remunerative prices, distribution of food-grains to the consumers, particularly, the vulnerable sections of the society at affordable prices and maintenance of food buffers for food security and price stability. The instruments for food management are the Minimum Support Price (MSP) and Central Issue Price (CIP). The focus is on incentivizing farmers by ensuring fair value for their produce through the Minimum Support Price mechanism, distribution of food-grains at subsidized rates to 6.52 crore BPL families, covering all households at the risk of hunger under Antyodaya Anna Yojana (AAY), establishing grain banks in chronically food-scarce areas and strengthening the Public Distribution System (PDS). The nodal agency which undertakes procurement, distribution and storage of food-grains is the Food Corporation of India (FCI). Procurement at MSP is an open-ended, while distribution is governed by the scale of allocation and its off-take by the beneficiaries.

Challenges and Outlook

The agriculture sector faces challenges on various fronts. On the supply side, the yield of most crops has not improved significantly and in some cases, fluctuated downwards. The scope for increase in the net sown area is limited and farm size has been shrinking. In the case of certain crops like sugarcane, extreme variability in the acreage and production over the years has been a matter of concern. On the other hand, in the case of pulses, production has just not kept pace with the requirement leading to a rise in prices given that its availability in the international markets is limited.

Therefore, there is clearly a need for a renewed focus on improving productivity, and at the same time, to step up the growth of allied activities and non-farm activities that can help to improve value addition.

■■■

Globalization in the New Century

To say that globalization has not encountered its share of dilemmas would be to fool ourselves. Other than the persistent headache it has caused, all other aspects of this twenty-first century system have encountered road blocks that portend potential disasters on a larger scale.

Still in its infancy, globalization has shown an unparalleled capability to reshape foreign economies and multinational business markets; the expansion of the Internet will only extend that influence, not only in economics but also in global politics.

At this crossroad of changing policies and technologies, we must be prudent about globalization's effect on foreign societies, identify the risks in expansion through the World Wide Web, and delineate between business and political partnerships. Now is the worst time to choose expediency over the ideals of fairness that we have long espoused.

Superficially, the US's endorsement of legitimate transnational trade agreements carries our message of fair and free trade, but we may be unintentionally overlooking the long term risks of global integration that depends on information technology (IT).

Many nations do not have equal access to the Internet, putting them at a disadvantage in a system more reliant on IT.

A microcosm of the emerging digital divide can be seen within our own borders, where the percentage of white people able to use computers greatly exceeds the percentage for African Americans. If such a disparity in the accessibility to IT were enlarged, as in the case of Africa versus its neighbours, many would fall into the widening digital abyss. After listening to Professor Vinod Aggarwal, Director of the APEC Study Center at UC Berkeley, talk at a recent Great Decisions session about the effects of globalization, I noticed that he had similar concerns about the possibility of people in lower socioeconomic levels being left further behind.

This, however, does not mean we should grind globalization to a screeching halt. The expansion of IT has promoted the exchange of free ideas in countries with oppressive governments, including China, where behind rigid authoritarian barriers, the Internet is opening new conduits of free speech.

Additionally, trade agreements are bringing the issue of human rights back on the table for discussion. I hope I can have a chance to hear more of what experts have to say about these challenges at this year's conference.

Expanding businesses online carries huge implications, and oftentimes, computer networks are enormous bubbles waiting to burst.

The "I Love You" computer virus, which crippled millions of computers worldwide last year, reaffirmed the volatility of the digital medium through which we are conducting more and more transactions.

A single Filipino hacker managed to spread chaos on a global scale; all he needed was an advanced knowledge of computer networks. In turn, such hackers can instigate a form of "online terrorism," disabling global markets by exploiting security flaws.

I feel that in this digital age, the public needs to be more informed about the vastly unexplored dangers of transferring sensitive information through the Internet.

One of the discussion topics for web development team has also been online security. As I have come to learn, the brick and mortar business model is becoming less appealing to entrepreneurs, but dealing primarily or solely in e-commerce elevates the risk of a massive shutdown due to hacking, with apparently little risk to the digital assailants themselves.

Illegal transactions can also be expedited online, another challenge for global law enforcement. The US, global trade groups, and Interpol need to address the problem together, something I am interested in hearing more about at Asilomar.

Since our business practices send strong messages about our policies (economic sanctions for our enemies and partnerships for our allies), the growing ambiguity in our ties to non-democratic states needs to be resolved.

Our support of China's entrance into the WTO needs to be followed by a reaffirmation in our opposition to China's human rights abuses. In an essay published in the school paper, I addressed the issue of unclear policies towards China in regards to China's WTO application. I have also written on the topic of human rights around the world in general.

Similar to China's problems, as African nations step up to do business with us, the US cannot condone the acts of gender abuse and ethnic cleansing that their governments ignore.

Economic policy shifts do not necessarily warrant

political policy changes, and if globalization is to fit our vision of fairness and freedom, we must continue to support policy towards that end. I am interested in gaining more insight into current US policy concerning its business ties around the world at the conference.

The shapers of globalization, as the keynote speaker William Maynes designated world superpowers at last year's Asilomar conference, now may impact global policies for decades to follow, making it crucial that we decide with conviction and purpose.

Expanding IT is a necessity, but we must transcend our Western perspective and truly examine the effects from a global standpoint if we are to be an effective leader in global integration.

Finding a compromise between our own interests and the needs of the rest of the globe is not a new challenge; it is simply a growing challenge.

■ ■ ■

Secularism in India

On paper, India is unquestionably a secular State with secure constitutional guarantees for all citizens. Yet, at a social and political level, secularism seems an abstraction. There is a serious contradiction between the secular goal of the Indian Constitution and the growing communalization of its polity.

Secularism cannot be defined without relating it to the socio-political context. What is true in the western context, may not be necessarily valid in Indian context and vice versa. Secularism, in philosophy and politics, is the rejection of religious and sacred forms and practices in favour of rational assessment and decision-making. In Europe and North America, secularism can be traced to the 18th-century Age of Enlightenment or Age of Reason.

Western dictionaries define "secularism" as the absence of religion, but Indian secularism means a profusion of religions, none of which is privileged by the State. Secularism in India does not mean irreligiousness, rather it means multi-religiousness.

However, the Indian society was very different from the European society in its socio-religious structure and could not, therefore, imitate the western model of secularism. It had to evolve its own model of secularism from its own experimental context.

Since there was not any struggle against any established religious authority, there was no question of any resentment against religion. Also, India was rich in pluralistic traditions, and mainly relied on them for developing its concept of secularism.

Thus, right from the beginning, Indian secularism drew its strength from pluralism. It was the religious community, rather than the religious authority, which mattered in the Indian context of secularism. The saner leaders of both the communities emphasized justice in power-sharing, without questioning the religious authority of either community.

In fact, the leaders of minority communities feared domination by the majority community and interference in their religious affairs. The leaders of the majority community, on the other hand, sought to assuage the feelings of minority communities by assuring them they would be free to follow their own religions.

Such leaders were called secular, while those of the majority community who resented unrestricted religious freedom for minorities were called communal. (a loose definition) Thus, in Indian secularism an anti-religious attitude did not play a part.

For Gandhiji, the basis of Hindu-Muslim unity was also a religion. The political unity, in his view, should also be based on one's religious duty to unite with other human beings. He wrote in the Harijan of July 6, 1947 that "....by trying to befriend Muslims I have only proved myself a true Hindu and have rightly served the Hindus and Hinduism. The essence of true religious teachings is that one should serve and befriend all". To strengthen his point he then goes on to quote a couplet—from Iqbal's famous poem *Naya Shivala*: "*Mazhab nahin sikhata aapas mein bayr rakhna*", meaning, religion does not teach us to bear ill-will towards one another.

Constitutional Concept

Differing views of national leaders meant that the form of secularism that found expression in the Constitution after independence was ambiguous. The result was that the Constitution sought to do several things. It made some allowance for the role played by religion, especially Hinduism, in Indian life. It also gave statutory recognition to minorities, thereby implicitly accepting the existence of a majority. It aimed to foster a common civic identity, but then compromised this by the provision of reserved seats in legislatures to Scheduled Castes and Scheduled Tribes (initially meant to last 10 years, no Parliament has contemplated doing away with this and its regular extension has become a formality).

Though our Constitution is secular, originally the word 'secular' found only a single casual mention in the document of 1950. The reference was to "economic, financial, political or other secular activity" in Article 25(2a) and the usage followed the standard dictionary meaning. It was only during the emergency in mid-seventies, during Congress party rule, that the words "secular and socialist" were added. The secular objective of the State was specifically expressed by inserting the word 'secular' in the Preamble of the Constitution (42nd Amendment) Act, 1976.

But the word 'secular' was not defined, although it was given official (not Constitutional but operational) expression in the State practice of maintaining equidistance from all religions, or paying equal respect to all religions, not favouring one at the cost of another.

Thus, the spirit of Indian secularism is not denial of

any religion or religious practice, but religio-cultural pluralism. It is certainly better than atheistic secularism as the latter does not admit the right of citizens to believe.

Some social scientists in India have argued that the serious threats to social tolerance and diversity in India today come either from an anti-democratic, majoritarian, ethnic nationalism or from a homogenizing and modernizing nation State, and the imposition of alien values on Indian society. Such theorists prefer a State which does not claim procedural neutrality and separation of State from religion but is, instead, guided by an encompassing indigenous culture, although they oppose the interpretations of Indian culture which are being marketed by right-wing forces today.

Minorities could be protected, they argue, by the tolerance and modes of coexistence which have evolved in the society over time, rather than by a modernizing nation State with alien values. The State should be prepared to devolve some of its powers and functions on to communities.

■ ■ ■

Re-Engineering and Total Quality Management (TQM)

Many organizations start with vague directives that have little clarity on what to do. Their successes are sporadic and likely to fail. Other organizations become victims of their own success. Their initial quality improvement teams are so successful that they rapidly create more teams, without the qualitative organization-wide changes necessary to sustain a permanent effort. Some of these changes are obvious—the companies must facilitate, recognize and encourage these teams. However, other qualitative changes also may be necessary. If these changes are not made, the TQM movement risks running into troubles.

Incremental Approach

In the incremental approach the companies deal with technical problems one at a time, without reviewing or changing any underlying "systems" issues, such as performance appraisal, profit sharing vs individual compensation, and organizational structure. Incremental approaches work best when senior management is unwilling to deal with these systems issues, when lower-level employees wish to experiment with TQM without senior management support, or when many in management are ambivalent towards TQM. Organizations can use approaches in "stealth" mode, where several quality improvement teams are quietly working without senior management's acknowledgement. These approaches are good for solving easy problems. Incremental approach can easily collapse when TQM "champions" leave the organization.

Incremental Changes-1

Option one the most frequently used models in implementing TQM, and perhaps the most wasteful of time and effort. Using this approach, every one in the company or a designated unit receives massive training (40-100 hours) in TQM, Statistical Process Control (SPC) and meeting management. After this training, employees in many are on their own.

In addition, because management does not tie training to implementation, natural work groups (people directly reporting to the same person), and cross-functional teams end up with only some of their members trained. Many people wait months before they use the training they were given.

The net result of this option is the loss of employee time due to too much training being given, employees feeling confused about the company's direction, and frustration at not using the training they received. Whatever success, these teams are limited by the structural barriers.

Incremental Change-2

Option two emphasizes: (1) defining the company's goals and objectives; (2) selecting quality improvement projects tied to those goals; (3) training only the members of the process improvement team with just enough training, just before they use it; and (4) providing on-going support of each team's efforts.

The result of using option two is a more sharply defined effort than in option 1, with a much greater chance that the quality improvement team's efforts will directly relate to the company's quality goals, and a greater sense of accomplishment will be there among team members.

As with option one, these teams' successes will be limited by the structural barriers the company has, i.e., compensation, organizational structure, performance appraisal, etc.

The Structural (Re-Engineering) Approach

The structural approach to implementing TQM deals initially and directly with the systems barriers described above. Using this approach, senior management forms a steering committee, who then designate a design team made of a diagonal slice of the company. This design team then assesses the company's culture, systems and environment, and develops recommendations for the steering committee. Such recommendations can include self-directed work teams, profit-based pay, pay for knowledge, and reorganizing the company away from the "functional stove-pipes" of manufacturing, engineering, sales and service, towards a more product, customer or geographically based orientation.

The chief advantages to this approach are: (1) dealing with major issues up-front, rather than avoiding them; (2) changing aspects of the company that will have a substantial effect on productivity; and (3) demonstrating that management is serious about quality.

Disadvantages include the need to be open and honest with employees from the beginning (if that is a disadvantage), and dealing head-on with issues that many in management may have trouble changing: their own management style, their own pay, and their own power.

■■■

Infrastructure: The Key to Rapid Growth

Like most of the developing countries, Indian Economy is also a diversified and resilient in nature. Similarly, like most of the developing countries, huge sums of funds are being spent on the development of infrastructure, both in the private as well as in the public sectors. But, it is felt that the infrastructure spending is shorter than what is ideally required for achieving the required higher growth rate. As per the estimation of the Planning Commission of India, the total requirement of funds for financing the infrastructure requirements during the Eleventh Five Year Plan (2007-12) is to the tune of USD 500 billion, which is about 2.5 times of the funds provided for this purpose during the Tenth Five Year Plan.

Realizing that the government may not be able to fund the huge requirement for infrastructure projects required to be taken up for rapid growth of the economy, the Union government and various State governments have come up with the required Public-Private Partnership (PPP) framework to facilitate the private participation in the infrastructure sector in a big way. The government has also asked the Infrastructure Investment Finance Company to earmark a corpus of over 8.15 billion US dollars for this purpose.

This is in addition to $320 billion to be spent by the government for the up-gradation of sea ports, railroads, highways and airports over the next about 15 years.

A massive 494 billion dollar investment is proposed in the Eleventh Five-Year Plan (2007-12), which would increase the share of infrastructure investment in this sector from 5 per cent of the GDP at the beginning of Eleventh Plan to 9 per cent during the Plan. This massive investment in the infrastructure sector is envisaged through huge doses of public spendings through several flagship national programmes, as well as through active participation of the private sector in this gigantic effort.

To facilitate PPP in infrastructure sectors, the government has not only introduced the model concession agreements but also permitted increased percentages of Foreign Direct Investment (FDI) in various sectors.

Major expansion of the infrastructure in the sub-sectors like railways, ports, civil aviation, road, power, telecommunications and housing is planned to be achieved during the plan period.

Urban infrastructure is targeted to be strengthened through the Jawaharlal Nehru National Urban Renewable Mission, while the general rural infrastructure is proposed to be up-graded through implementation of national programmes like Bharat Nirman, Rajiv Gandhi Gramin Vidyutikaran Yojana, and National Rural Health Mission etc.

Private Participation

Policy makers realise that the basic goal of inclusive development laid down for the Eleventh Five Year Plan may not be achieved if the basic infrastructure facilities are not available in the urban as well as rural areas of the country. In this regard, the participation of the private sector is considered to be very important.

Partnership with the private sector had been continuing in the country during the past several years but there was no defined uniform policy and legal framework till recently.

The government of India has setup a PPP cell in the Ministry of Finance, Department of Economic Affairs. It is also felt that many PPP projects may not be economically viable but are essentially required to be executed. For such projects, Viability Gap Funding (VGF) Scheme has been introduced.

This is a special facility aimed at supporting such infrastructure projects which are economically and socially justifiable but are not commercially viable.

Under the VGF Scheme, upfront assistance upto 20 per cent of the project cost can be sanctioned as a grant for such PPP projects.

No facilitation is complete without making institutional arrangements for financing. The Government of India has setup India Infrastructure Finance Company Ltd (IIFCL) as a wholly government-owned company to facilitate long-term funding of infrastructure projects. IIFCL provides direct financing, as well as refinancing of such projects in public, private or PPP sector.

The government has also paid special attention towards the capacity building at the Central and State levels.

Capacity building needs include training of the key personnel, development of standard toolkits, Model Concession Agreements, development of Project Manuals, preparation of standard bidding documents, consultancy support and project preparation manuals. This effort is also being supported by the Asian Development Bank.

Over the past three to four years, the government of India has worked towards creating institutional framework to facilitate it.

Precursor to Rapid Growth

Infrastructure development has been identified as an effective tool for taking the economy out of the effects of global recession. There has been stiff increase in the proposed expenditure for infrastructure projects particularly in the rural areas. A 31 per cent increase has been proposed in the interim Budget 2009-10 for Bharat Nirman programme, aimed at strengthening the rural infrastructure in the country.

This would not only increase the economic activity in the countryside but would also provide the rural people with the required infrastructure and increased employment opportunities.

One of the ambitious ongoing infrastructure projects is the Golden Quadrilateral Project, which is aimed at improving the road infrastructure on the highways/expressways connecting major cities of the country. The Project, on completion, would connect the metropolitan cities of Delhi, Mumbai, Bangalore, Chennai and Kolkata with expressways.

It is the largest expressway project of the country, aimed at constructing 5,846 kilometres of six/four lane express highways at a cost of Rs 60,000 crore. Its North-South and East-West sections are nearing completion while the work on other sections is going on.

Road infrastructure, world class telecommunications, availability of efficient sea ports and airports, capacity creation in electricity generation and strong rural and urban infrastructure are some of the areas identified for the improvement by the policy-makers.

After the planning stage, it is now the implementation stage and it is expected that within next five to ten years, India would have all the world class infrastructure facilities available.

In addition to creation of sustainable infrastructure in the country, the government effort would also result in ensuring huge doses of investment into the economy, including the rural economy, at a time when most of the western and developed markets are reeling under the influence of worldwide recession.

Investment in this sector has ensured that the economy grew at 7 per cent during the previous financial year, when the world growth rate was around one per cent. During the current fiscal also, when the world economy is likely to record zero growth rate, Indian Economy may still record some reasonable growth rate.

■ ■ ■

Rich-Poor Divide: Can It Be Bridged?

Despite the high growth rate of the economy, in absolute terms India still is a low income economy, with its per capita income at a level less than $500 per annum. Low per capita income is a pointer towards the existing sharp divide between India's wealthiest and poorest sections of society. Out of the total population, about 26 million people live below poverty line and 35 per cent out of this group, also classified as the poorest of the poor, having income level of less than $1 per day.

As per 2001 Census, about 78 million people in the country were living without a home and more than that number were holed up in urban slums. The number of the poor living in the country is more than the poor living in any other country of the world.

Despite the above socio-economic problems plaguing the Indian society, post-reforms period has been marked by high growth rate, placing the country among the front runners in the race for highest growth in the world. During the past five years, India has been second after China in terms of the growth rate achieved.

India's Information Technology (IT) industry, services, manufacturing and automobile sectors have been booming. The urban areas, particularly the metropolitan cities, have been the centres of growth. Industrial centres have also been the hubs of economic activity and the income levels in the country are on the rise.

During the past decade, the foreign sector in the country had also been performing extremely well and the policy of globalization had paid rich dividends, with the foreign sector, registering over 20 per cent growth in the past several years. Without taking away the credit from the liberalization policy, the resilience of the Indian economy must also be given its due credit for outstanding achievements.

Unfortunately, the spurt in economic activity in the country and increase in the growth rate over the past few years has not been able to make a discernible dent on the problem of poverty, deprivation and exploitation of the downtrodden. The divide between the rich and the poor has now become a tangible reality. There are more Indian billionaires in the Forbes list than ever before. But the number of the poor and hungry is also not decreasing. The growth centres are encircled by the group of underprivileged people whose basic needs are still to be met.

During this era of rapid growth, the problems of unequal and skewed distribution of economic resources and the fruits of growth have surfaced.

In addition to the economic divide between the rich and the poor, the digital divide between various regions of the country has also become an important issue. It has been admitted by the government policy makers that the growth rate in the rural areas has been quite sluggish despite high growth rate in the urban centres.

Economic activity in the rural areas has not been able to pick up to match the rapid growth of the cities. The result is that in the hope of getting better employment and growth opportunities a large number of people are migrating to the cities every year.

Rural economy is largely comprised of the agriculture and allied activities. The growth rate of the agricultural sector has been between 2 to 4 per cent over the past couple of decades, while the rest of the economy is growing at the rate of around 8 per cent. It implies that increase in incomes in the rural sector has been almost one-third of the average growth of incomes in the country. Resultantly, the rural economy has emerged as a poor cousin of the urban and industrial sectors and the existing yawning gap has actually increased further.

The above does not imply that all is well in the urban sector as a whole. Urban areas have their own set of problems and inequalities resulting in what is known as urban-urban divide. The urban problems in India are not different. With about 300 million people living in 5,000 cities and towns, the urban population cries for more care, investment in urban infrastructure and basic civic amenities.

About 40% of the urban population in India lives in 60 metropolitan urban agglomerations. As per one estimate of the government, about 65 million urban people live in slums and squatter settlements in these agglomerations. It is estimated that the urban population of the country would increase to 468 million by the year 2020. This poses a Herculean task to the cities in terms of improvements in civic infrastructure, housing, basic amenities and employment opportunities.

The current situation in most of the cities and towns is pathetic. Mumbai, Delhi and Kolkata are the main business and growth centres in the country.

In addition, cities like Bengaluru and Hyderabad are the hub centres of the IT revolution in the country. But these very cities have their darker side as well. There is a huge population of urban poor and slum dwellers living there. Water supply and sanitation is serious problem and solid waste collection and its safe disposal is something that requires a major national initiative.

The variation in the income levels in the cities has also created a kind of dichotomy in the society and the vertical split in the society is a matter of serious concern for the sociologists as well as the economists.

Bridging the Gap

Equitable growth of the economy is the ultimate goal and every government must strive hard to achieve this goal. Indian Constitution, through the Directive Principles of State Policy entrusts the responsibility of equitable distribution of economic resources to the government policies.

Globalization cannot snatch away the basic right of decent living from the poor and the downtrodden. It is the duty and responsibility of the government to take immediate measures for bridging the widening gap, which requires pragmatic policies aimed at redistributive justice on sustainable basis.

Government of India has already launched an ambitious programme aimed at stimulating the economic activities in the rural areas. Known as Bharat Nirman, this new initiative is expected to pump in huge sums of public expenditure in the development of rural infrastructure of the country.

Two more flagship programmes, called "Sarv Siksha Abhiyan" and "National Rural Health Mission", are being implemented which aim at bringing in qualitative as well as numerical improvement in the education and healthcare sectors, particularly in the rural areas.

To take care of the urban-urban divide, another ambitious programme called Jawaharlal Nehru National Urban Renewal Mission is being implemented in 66 major cities of the country under which a lot of funds are being spent to upgrade the urban infrastructure, housing and service delivery mechanism.

In addition to the above initiatives, the government has to ensure distributive justice through its taxation and other economic policies. Due attention is required to be paid to the education sector in the rural areas so that the people living there are able to get the best possible education to compete with their urban counterparts.

Healthcare and sanitation facilities need a total upgrade in the entire country. Special attention of the government is required to be focused on stepping up the economic activities in the rural areas so that the rural incomes experience the required upsurge and the existing gap is bridged to some extent. Divide in the early stages of development is a global phenomenon but it must not be allowed to perpetuate beyond reasonable limit.

∎∎∎

Financial Sector Reforms in India

The period immediately after independence posed a major challenge to the country. Due to centuries of exploitation at the hands of foreign powers, there were very high levels of deprivation in the economy—both social as well as economic. To take up the Herculean task of rapid growth with socio-economic justice, the country adopted the system of planned economic development after independence. Due to paucity of economic resources and limitations of availability of capital for investment, the government also came up with the policy of setting up public enterprises in almost every field.

The fiscal activism adopted by the government resulted in large doses of public expenditures for which not only the revenues of the government were utilized but the government also resorted to borrowing at concessional rates, which kept the financial markets underdeveloped. The growth of fiscal deficit also continued unabated year after year. Complex structure of interest rates was a resultant outcome of this system.

Nationalization of major commercial banks in the late sixties and early seventies provided the government with virtually the complete control over the direction of the bank credit. The emphasis was mainly on control and regulation and the market forces had very limited role to play.

The economic system was working to the satisfaction of the government. The social indicators were gradually improving and the number of people below poverty line also declined steadily. The only problem area had been that the growth rate of the economy had been very low, and till late seventies, the growth rate of the GDP was hovering around 3.5 per cent per annum. It was only during mid-eighties that the growth rate touched 5 percentage points.

The situation became difficult by the eighties. Financial system was considerably stretched and artificially directed and concessional availability of credit with respect to certain sectors resulted in distorting the interest rate mechanism.

Lack of professionalism and transparency in the functioning of the public sector banks led to increasing burden of non-performance of their assets.

Late eighties and early nineties were characterised by fluid economic situation in the country. War in the Middle East had put tremendous pressure on the dwindling foreign exchange reserves of the country. The country witnessed the worst shortages of the petroleum products. High rate of inflation was another area of serious concern.

Most of the economic ailments had resulted due to over regulation of the economy. The international lending and assisting agencies were ready to extend assistance but with the condition that the country went in for structural reforms, decontrols and deregulation, allowing increased role for the market forces of demand and supply.

The precarious economic conditions left the country with no alternative other than acceptance of the conditions for introducing the reforms.

Post Reforms

Rationalization of the taxes has already taken place on

the basis of the recommendations of Raja Challiah Committee Report during mid-nineties.

The government has been able to tighten its fiscal management through the FRBMA and the continuing increase in the fiscal deficit has been contained significantly. Reforms in the external sector management have yielded results in the form of increased foreign capital inflows in terms of Foreign Direct Investment (FDI), Foreign Institutional Investment (FII) and the exchange rate has also represent true international value of Indian rupee vis-à-vis hard global currencies.

The primitive foreign exchange regulation regime controlled by FERA has been replaced by a liberalized foreign exchange rate management system introduced by FEMA. Introduction of such a modern management law was perhaps a pre-condition for allowing FDI and FII. In 1993, the RBI issued guidelines to allow the private sector banks to enter the banking sector in the country, a virtual reversal of the policy of bank nationalisation. Foreign banks were also given more liberal entry.

The thrust of the monetary policy after the introduction of the process of reforms has been able to develop several instruments of efficient financial management. A Liquidity Adjustment Facility (LAF) was introduced in June 2000 to precisely modulate short-term liquidity and signal short-term interest rates.

A lot of reliance is being placed on indirect instruments of monetary policy. Strengthening and upgradation of the institutional, technological and physical infrastructure in the financial markets has also improved the financial framework in the country.

Economy and Reforms

The introduction of financial sector reforms has provided the economy with a lot of resilience and stability. The average annual growth rate of the economy during the post-reform period has been more than 6 per cent, which was unimaginable a decade before that.

The economy withstood boldly the Asian economic crisis of 1997-98. Even the economic sanctions by the US and other developed countries after the nuclear testing did not affect the economy to the extent apprehended. The current global slowdown and sub-prime crisis affecting the banking system all over the world has not impacted the Indian Economy to that extent.

Banking and insurance sectors are booming. While the private and foreign banks are giving stiff but healthy competition to the public sector banks, resulting in overall improvements in the banking services in the country, the insurance sector has also witnessed transformation. The consumer is a gainer with the availability of much better and diversified insurance products.

The stock exchanges in the country are in the process of adopting the best practices all over the world. The RBI has also been able to control and regulate effectively the operations and growth of the Non-Banking Financial Companies (NBFCs) in the country.

A few changes which are on the anvil pertain to the legal provisions relating to fiscal and budget management, public debt, deposits, insurance etc. As per the Finance Minister, future reforms by making legal changes also pertain to banking regulations, Companies Act, Income Tax, Bankruptcy, negotiable instruments etc.

But there are certain issues that call for more cautious approach towards the financial sector reforms in the future. The social sector indicators—like availability of doctor per 1000 population, availability of health institutions, quality of elementary education, literacy rate, particularly among the females—are some of the areas of serious concern.

Countries like China, Indonesia and even Sri Lanka are much better than India in most of the social sector indicators.

Despite being among the most rapidly developing economies of the world, the literacy rate and poverty percentage are two biggest embarrassments and the country still languishes at 128th position in the Human Development Index of the UNDP, where it is virtually stagnating for the last about five years. Further, the systems should also be able to check any unusual rise in prices to protect the common man from inflation.

■ ■ ■

Role of Banks and Financial Institutions in Economy

Money lending in one form or the other has evolved along with the history of the mankind. Even in the ancient times there are references to the moneylenders. Shakespeare also referred to 'Shylocks' who made unreasonable demands in case the loans were not repaid in time along with interest. Indian history is also replete with the instances referring to indigenous money lenders, *Sahukars* and Zamindars involved in the business of money lending by mortgaging the landed property of the borrowers.

Independence of the country heralded a new era in the growth of modern banking. Many new commercial banks came up in various parts of the country.

As the modern banking network grew, the government began to realise that the banking sector was catering only to the needs of the well-to-do and the capitalists. The interests of the poorer sections as well as those of the common man were being ignored.

In 1969, Indian Government took a historic decision to nationalise 14 biggest private commercial banks. A few more were nationalised after a couple of years.

This resulted in transferring the ownership of these banks to the State and the Reserve Bank of India could then issue directions to these banks to fund the national programmes, the rural sector, the plan priorities and the priority sector at differential rate of interest.

This resulted in providing fillip the banking facilities

to the rural areas, to the under-privileged and the downtrodden. It also resulted in financial inclusion of all categories of people in almost all the regions of the country.

However, after almost two decades of bank nationalisation some new issues became contextual. The service standards of the public sector banks began to decline.

Their profitability came down and the efficiency of the staff became suspect. Non-performing assets of these banks began to rise. The wheel of time had turned a full circle by early nineties and the government after the introduction of structural and economic reforms in the financial sector, allowed the setting up of new banks in the private sector.

The new generation private banks have now established themselves in the system and have set new standards of service and efficiency. These banks have also given tough but healthy competition to the public sector banks.

Modern Day Role

Banking system and the Financial Institutions play very significant role in the economy. First and foremost is in the form of catering to the need of credit for all the sections of society. The modern economies in the world have developed primarily by making best use of the credit availability in their systems.

An efficient banking system must cater to the needs of high end investors by making available high amounts of capital for big projects in the industrial, infrastructure and service sectors.

At the same time, the medium and small ventures must also have credit available to them for new investment and expansion of the existing units. Rural sector in a country like India can grow only if cheaper credit is available to the farmers for their short and medium term needs.

Credit availability for infrastructure sector is also extremely important. The success of any financial system can be fathomed by finding out the availability of reliable and adequate credit for infrastructure projects.

Fortunately, during the past about one decade there has been increased participation of the private sector in infrastructure projects.

The banks and the financial institutions also cater to another important need of the society i.e. mopping up small savings at reasonable rates with several options. The common man has the option to park his savings under a few alternatives, including the small savings schemes introduced by the government from time to time and in bank deposits in the form of savings accounts, recurring deposits and time deposits. Another option is to invest in the stocks or mutual funds.

In addition to the above traditional role, the banks and the financial institutions also perform certain new-age functions which could not be thought of a couple of decades ago.

The facility of internet banking enables a consumer to access and operate his bank account without actually visiting the bank premises. The facility of ATMs and the credit/debit cards has revolutionised the choices available with the customers. The banks also serve as alternative gateways for making payments on account of income-tax and online payment of various bills like the telephone, electricity and tax. The bank customers can also invest their funds in various stocks or mutual funds straight from their bank accounts. In the modern day economy, where people have no time to make these payments by standing in queue, the service provided by the banks is commendable.

While the commercial banks cater to the banking needs of the people in the cities and towns, there is another category of banks that looks after the credit and banking needs of the people living in the rural areas, particularly the farmers.

Regional Rural Banks (RRBs) have been sponsored by many commercial banks in several States. These banks, along with the cooperative banks, take care of the farmer-specific needs of credit and other banking facilities.

Future

Till a few years ago, the government largely patronized the small savings schemes in which not only the interest rates were higher, but the income tax rebates and incentives were also in plenty. The bank deposits, on the other hand, did not entail such benefits.

As a result, the small savings were the first choice of the investors. But for the last few years the trend has been reversed. The small savings, the bank deposits and the mutual funds have been brought at par for the purpose of incentives under the income tax. Moreover, the interest rates in the small savings schemes are no longer higher than those offered by the banks.

Banks today are free to determine their interest rates within the given limits prescribed by the RBI. It is now easier for the banks to open new branches. But the banking sector reforms are still not complete. A lot more is required to be done to revamp the public sector banks.

Mergers and amalgamation is the next measure on the agenda of the government. The government is also preparing to disinvest some of its equity from the PSU banks. The option of allowing foreign direct investment beyond 50 per cent in the Indian banking sector has also been under consideration.

Banks and financial Institutions have played major role in the economic development of the country and most of the credit-related schemes of the government to uplift the poorer and the under-privileged sections have been implemented through the banking sector. The role of the banks has been important, but it is going to be even more important in the future.

■■■

Barack Hussein Obama

Obama's overblown media image has blurred the perceptions of the proverbial common man. In spite of the fact that most facts of his life are known to the public, it is difficult to understand him as a political leader and to say definitely, at this starting point of his Presidency, what kind of President he would make. He has been compared to Lincoln, Roosevelt and J.F. Kennedy, but these comparisons appear invidious because all of them were white Americans; nor can his realization of the American Dream be called a rag to riches story.

To a perceptive observer, he would look like a mulatto character from Faulkner's novels who suddenly has woken up into the twenty–first century multicultural America and remembers no nightmares of the reality of his 18th or 19th century past of racial discrimination and historic humiliation.

He is the first African-American to hold the office of the President of the United States. He, more than anything else, represents the mixed, educated, immigrant middle-class of the present-day USA.

Obama is a graduate of Columbia University and Harvard Law School, where he was the first African-American president of the Harvard Law Review. He worked as a community organizer, and practiced as a civil rights attorney in Chicago before serving three terms in the Illinois Senate from 1997 to 2004. He also taught Constitutional Law at the University of Chicago Law School from 1992 to 2004. He was defeated in the US

Congress elections 2000, but got elected to the Senate in November 2004. In July 2004, as a Democratic minority member in the 109th Congress he helped make legislation to control conventional weapons and for greater public accountability in federal funds spending. He also made official trips to Eastern Europe, the Middle East and Africa.

During the 110th Congress he contributed to legislation on lobbying and electoral fraud, climate change, nuclear terrorism, care for US military personnel returning from combat assignments in Iraq and Afghanistan.

Thus, he is not entirely the creation of the media. Had he been purely white, instead of half-white half-black as he is, his rise would not have attracted such exaggerated media attention.

How long the honey-moon with the media will last is hard to say. He faces the enormous task of putting the derailed economy on course and sustaining the vast but doubtful military involvements of USA abroad, especially in Asia. As President, he will also have to rework political, economic and diplomatic equations with almost every important country of the world.

The spell of relief from the outgoing toxic Bush administration will be over soon. The obvious historical significance of an African-American taking over as President of the United States, "a polity substantially founded on the genocide of one race and the slave labour of another", will also soon start glowering at all Americans—implications will be global.

Obama's sudden rise, no doubt, is the outcome of racial politics. He has certainly benefited from the legacy of the civil rights and black liberation movements of the 1960s, led by Martin Luther King Jr. and Malcom X, both of whom got assassinated. So many others died in these movements.

These events have left a great impact on American society and transformed large segments of its people. That social transformation is believed to have been responsible for making 66 per cent of those between the age of 18 and 29, and 52 per cent of those in the 30-44 age group vote for Mr Obama.

Surprisingly, he is neither a product of that legacy nor one to associate with its militant ideological stance. Yet, he is its absolute beneficiary.

Obama's middle Muslim name created some early troubles but repeated assertions of his deep Christian faith finally overcame the public doubts. He strictly prohibited his campaign staff from wearing any visibly Islamic gear, both in public or on television.

He made it a point to visit churches and synagogues but never a mosque, ignoring the unsolicited counsel of important newspapers like *The New York Times* and *International Herald Tribune*.

His foreign policy postures also reflected a similar stance. Obama criticized the UN for permitting the Iranian President Ahmadinejad to address the UN General Assembly even when US national agencies confirmed that Iran has no nuclear weapons programme.

He has reiterated quite a few times his intention to use all American power, including military force, to stop Iran's nuclear programme.

Almost in Bush-like tones, he has expressed his unwavering commitment to escalate the war in Afghanistan and widening the scope of US bombing in northwestern Pakistan, with or without the consent of the Pakistanis. To that extent, he has indicated continuity of Bush administration's military unilateralism.

His pursuit of support from Israel and the Israeli lobby in the US has been persistent. Uri Avnery, the veteran Israeli writer and peace activist, described Mr Obama's appearance at the American-Israeli Public Affairs Committee (AIPAC) as one that "broke all records for obsequiousness and fawning".

He stopped former President Jimmy Carter from speaking at the Democratic Party Convention for fear of a backlash from the Israeli lobby; this was described as "a cynical kind of pragmatism".

Mr Obama's stirring populist rhetoric during the campaign and use of words like "Change" and "Hope" and undulating chant, "Yes, We can", boosted a demoralized nation and supercharged its younger people.

He made broad promises to rebuild a crestfallen nation—its infrastructure, its education and health systems and to revamp its tax structure to favour families earning less than $250,000 a year. He forged a cross-racial coalition of the young, the poor and the unemployed, as also the middle classes imparting to his campaign—a progressive veneer in a nation soaked in neo-liberalism.

So the Right Wing labelled him as a "socialist" but to no effect. For Obama, winning the elections proved easier than subduing Hillary Clinton. The financial meltdown too came just at the right moment to turn the tables on John McCain.

Obama's campaign raised far more money than any other US presidential candidates in history, not all from small donors, contrary to his campaigners' claim. Fewer than 2,600 contributors to Mr McCain campaign fund were "chief executives", nearly 6,000 of Mr Obama's contributors were listed as chief executive officers.

Washington lobbyists and lawyers, the communication industry and the electronics industry, healthcare-related private interests, nuclear and pharmaceutical industries and all kinds of big business made huge contributions. Lobbyists alone gave $37 million. Will they and other big donors not be rewarded?

His previous record in politics shows that he made a speech opposing the impending Iraq war in 2002, before he came even into the Illinois Senate but he voted in favour of every war appropriation bill during the Bush administration.

He edited the Harvard Law Review, taught law at Chicago University, and was a civil rights lawyer before coming into politics, but as a Senator he, without compunction, voted for the Patriot Act 2, notorious for extreme curtailment of civil liberties in recent US history.

He, along with Mr McCain, voted in favour of the bailout plan that gifts hundreds of billions of dollars to the very financial institutions who caused the infamous meltdown. As President-elect he urged the Bush administration to bail out General Motors as well.

Mr Obama has been advocating a military policy that is incompatible with the investments he has proposed to re-build America's failing physical and social infrastructure.

Thus, somewhere there is a quirk in his leadership—projected as pacifist and progressive.

Finally, we have to consider the Indo-US relationship under Mr Obama? The basics of the new Indo-US equation were formulated under Mr Clinton and not under Mr Bush. A far-reaching military alliance for the Indian Ocean and beyond; the US-Israel-India axis for West Asia; the nuclear trade are likely to be pursued by Obama, though without flair. There could be some pressure to sign the Comprehensive Test Ban Treaty (CTBT) but that will not endanger nuclear trade.

Obama represents a declining West and America. For an assurance of his doubtfully great presidency, he can only look backward to the USA's past glory. America is a futurist nation, but if Obama looks forward, he will only see an Asia Rising—not a very comfortable thought even for an African-American President of the USA!

■■■

Reforms in Governance and Poverty Alleviation

Governance is the exercise of economic, political and administrative authority to manage a country's affairs at all levels. It consists of the whole set of processes, mechanisms and institutions through which the citizens express their interests, exercise their rights, meet their obligations and sink their differences. No amount of developmental effort can bring in improvements in the quality of life of the citizens without improving the governance standards.

Conversely, if the power of the State is misused, the poorer sections of the society are most likely to suffer. Poor governance, thus, perpetuates poverty and severely hinders the efforts to reduce it. It is understood all over the world that strengthening of governance is an essential precondition to improve the lives of the poor.

Initial years after independence were marked by the euphoria of emancipation from the foreign rulers. The entire politico-economic system was in the process of witnessing a host of changes, based on the experience gained.

Various new statutes were brought in and the Constitution was also amended several times as per the changing and felt needs of the society, notwithstanding the political angles and desired populism by the ruling political parties.

Successive governments also strived to ensure upliftment of the poor and the downtrodden. While several schemes and programmes were framed for the betterment of the socially and educationally weaker sections, the women and the children, the government also introduced several schemes aimed at alleviation of poverty, as it was clearly understood that the country may not be able to achieve the goal of rapid develop- ment unless the poorer sections of the society also experienced increase in their incomes and became part of the mainstream bandwagon of economic development.

It has been experienced by the country over the past six decades that despite billions of rupees pumped in the rural sector since independence, through various schemes and programmes, the desired outcomes have not been achieved. The number of people below poverty line has declined but at a very slow pace and the results have not been commensurate with the quantum of funds invested by the government.

Even from social point of view, it has been proved through many studies that there have been significant leakages in the expenditure made for the welfare of the weaker sections of society.

All this is strong pointer to the fact that the governance in the country needs improvement to achieve an improved delivery system. Over the last few decades, successive Five-Year Plans have tried to introduce certain reforms through their broad-based objectives. Democratic decentralization was achieved through the strengthened Panchayati Raj System and the resultant social empowerment has been one major initiative in this direction.

The focus of other initiatives has been on transparency, people's participation, civil service reforms, rationalisation of government schemes, improving access to formal justice, improvements in land administration and introduction of information technology as a key to good governance.

Enactment of the Right to Information Act has been a major breakthrough in bringing transparency in the government functioning and empowerment of the citizens of the country. Several economic reforms have also been taken up in the recent years.

Though the policy-makers may be taking a lot of credit for all these actions, yet the above governance initiatives are not sufficient and a lot more remains to be done. Maintenance of law and order of the desired level remains a pipe dream in many States. The general perception is that the law and order machinery is generally inefficient, tardy and unresponsive.

Corruption is rampant, undermining economic growth, distorting competition, and disproportionately hurting the poor and marginalised citizens. Criminalization of politics continues unchecked, with money and muscle power playing a major role in elections. In general, there is high degree of volatility in the society on account of unfulfilled expectations and poor service delivery.

Future Goals

Any attempt towards reforms in governance in the future must focus on two things—the fulfilment of human potential and rapid economic growth. The broad objective of realising human potential includes the prevention of human sufferings, ensuring human dignity, providing access to justice and making available equal opportunity to all so that every citizen becomes a fulfilled and productive human being. Rapid economic growth, on the other hand, would result in realising the country's real potential and provide India with an opportunity to play rightful role to protect the interests of the people of the country, while ensuring that the people living below poverty line also get their due share in the growing prosperity of the country.

The role of the State in basic services needs to be clearly defined and emphasized. Ensuring access to speedy and efficient justice, protecting rights of the citizens, enforcing rule of law and maintaining public order are all inseparable and form the basic foundation of a civilised society, as well as that of the democracy. The deficiencies in this vital area need to be plugged through judicial and police reforms, better participation of citizens in governance.

Based on the past experience and best practices, we need to redesign our delivery mechanisms in the education sector in an innovative manner and deploy the nation's finest talent to man in these sectors. Inadequate and poor quality of school education is the bane of Indian society today. Except in case of some better institutions of higher and technical/professional education, higher education too is not very successful in promoting excellence and producing quality service providers, dynamic leaders, result-oriented managers and long-term wealth creators.

Urban management involves much more than resource allocation for infrastructure and poses formidable challenges of governance, considering high rate of urbanization and future projections for the same in the country. Management of power distribution through active involvement of people in a consumer-friendly way is more of a governance issue than a tariff problem.

Social security is a relatively new and emerging area

of State activity to which the administrative system must respond with sensitivity. This would directly improve the lives of the poor. The recent enforcement of the employment guarantee law in the entire country and the efforts in the pipeline to provide a measure of social security to the unorganized sector workers can address the special challenges posed in social security, particularly for the economically weaker sections. But a lot more is required to be done.

In any system, the quality of public servants is critical in determining the outcomes of governance inputs. We have well-established procedures for initial recruitment of civil servants in India. But there is a growing concern that our administration in general has become unresponsive, rigid and inward-looking. While the bureaucracy responds to crisis situations with efficacy, complacency results in failure to deal with 'normal' situations, which is evident in most cases. The complex challenges of modern administration in critical sectors like police administration, justice delivery, education, healthcare, transportation, land management, infrastructure, skill promotion, employment generation and urban management need special attention. These areas impact the lives of all sections of the society, particularly the lives of the poorer sections.

There are no two views that the governance has been a weak link in our quest for rapid development with equity. The country has an impressive governance structure and several important successes to credit. But we need to consolidate the gains already made and venture into the virgin but vital areas of reforms in governance.

■■■

Self-Communication Solves Personal Problems

Psychiatrists have caught up with Socrates and cashed on this technique. They employ this technique as a powerful self-communication instrument to bring about personality change and improvement. The troubled person just talks (to himself) while the psychiatrist records his expression—verbal as well as facial. He also carefully watches his body language.

The aim is not to advise him but to give him an opportunity to unburden his mind, to see his own thinking in a new perspective, and thus find solutions to his problems.

Here is one example from my own life. I was at cross-roads of my career, after a spell of unemployment. It so happened that I got three offers almost simultaneously.

These were PR job in Haryana government, a similar job in a Haryana University, and a lecturer's job in Punjab University. I debated the dilemma of job-thinking in my mind for a couple of days, and opted for the PU job.

It was self-communication that helped to resolve the dilemma. The role of the self can be adequately played by a good listener.

One person who is truly understanding, who listens to you as you struggle with your problems, can change your outlook on the world.

Few people go to professional psychiatrists with their problems, but many take their troubles to friends and some to relatives. When a person in trouble knows that he has a good listener he shares his thoughts fully, which makes it easier to solve his problems. As he talks he finds a solution to his problem himself.

The emphatic listening is described as non-directive. The word refers to the reaction that a listener should present to a talker who is trying to discuss his own problems.

Another way of putting it is to say that the listener makes an effort to understand what is said, but does not give direction.

The listener realizes that he is a sounding board. The talker does not want advice. He wants to talk freely so that he can listen to his own thoughts as they are put into words.

With this opportunity to hear himself speak, he is able to furnish his own advice. In brief, the good listener accepts that is said, tries to understand it, and above all, makes no judgements.

Empathic understanding with a person, not about him, is an effective approach. It can bring about a major personality change.

If you want to find out how it is to listen without making evaluation judgements, test this experiment. The next time you find yourself in a heated discussion with your friend or spouse, let this rule be followed:

Each person can speak up for himself only after he has first restated the ideas and feelings of the previous speaker accurately and to the speaker's satisfaction.

This means that before presenting your own point of view, it would be necessary for you to achieve the other speaker's thoughts and feelings so well that you could summarise them for him.

Sounds simple, but you will discover that it is one of the most difficult things you have ever tried to do.

However, once you have been able to see the other's point of view, your own comment will have to be revised.

You will also find the emotions going out of the discussion, the differences being reduced, and those differences which remain being of a rational and an understandable sort.

Why is non-directive listening so difficult to accomplish? The answer lies in the fact that such listening requires a kind of courage that few of us have ever required.

When we listen to another person's ideas, we open ourselves up to the possibility that some of our own ideas are wrong.

Most of us fight for the change, especially when it has to do with altering our own thoughts. Therefore, when we listen, something from inside makes us want to fight for the change in our thinking that might be brought about by what we hear.

Hold on there, we are urged to say. You must be wrong. That isn't the way I think. And you are not going to change my mind. I won't allow it.

There is no sure formula for the kind of listening that can help people when they feel the very human desire to be heard. It depends too much on an attitude that must come from the inside of the listener.

No one can spell out a method by which you can become sympathetic and understanding to another person.

The following points will help in forming non-directive listenings:

Listen: Whenever you sense that someone is troubled or needs to talk, give him your time. Though it may seem like a waste of time to you, it seldom is.

If by listening, you can help him to clear his mind, it will also help in the communication between you and the person talking.

Also, there may come a time when you need a listener, and it is a fact that a good listener has little difficulty finding listeners.

Be attentive: If a verbal avalanche is launched, let it flow uninterrupted until it is exhausted.

Make every mental effort to understand what is said. Put yourself in the talker's place to understand what he says.

Verbal reactions: As the talker proceeds, use a series of eloquent and encouraging grunts: Humm, Uh-huh, Oh, or I see.

If the talker pauses, you should remain silent. Or nod your head, until talker starts again.

If he becomes unreasonable, you should restate what has just been said, putting it in the form of a question. Examples of such restatements might be: You really think life that? Or, you believe your mother-in-law is trying to ruin your marriage?

Probe not: There is a difference between willingness to listen and curiosity designed to dig for hidden information. The latter must be avoided. your purpose is not to obtain unwanted information.

Evaluate not: You should refrain from passing moral judgement upon what is said. In no case you should give an advice to the talker —even if he requests for it. Have faith in the ability of the troubled talker to solve his own problems.

You are witnessing an amazing human phenomenon. The person is talking things over with himself. If you do not inject yourself into his conversation, the chances are that the talker will work things out for himself.

The importance of what lies behind the need for listeners is important. An understanding of what happens when a person talks and another listens is found at the foundations of today's wellness psychotherapy. It is the therapatic value of communication. It works wonders in human relationships. Just know and follow the fundamentals.

The psychiatrist's most important tool is listening. A non-directive counselling, now practised more and more widely throughout business and industry, depends upon persons trained to listen quietly and objectively.

In most job interviews one basic approach is to let the candidate speak about himself. This provides a peep into his inner self, an interview is the real purpose of a view from inside.

Even in day-to-day living there is a way that you can communicate with yourself, but it requires the help of another individual, a listener, and a very good one.

If you find such a listener, he, in a sense, becomes a mirror that throws back a reflection of yourself.

The listener hears your words but, what is more important, you should hear yourself talking. If the listener remains active, but silent, giving you a chance to talk freely, thoughts from both the conscious and subconscious levels of your brain are put into words.

As a result you have the opportunity to hear from both parts of our brain speaking. Many times this result in self-communication you have been seeking all along. In effect, then you solve your own problems.

You don't have to spend enormous money or energy to be yourself. Just talk to yourself.

■ ■ ■

Importance of Self-Confidence

You can learn from many sources that you live in a world of your own making. That what you think tends to make your life. Since you are the master of your own thought life, and can choose what you think, you have it in your power to change your life from failure to success. If you are lacking in self-confidence, you can transform yourself and brim with supreme confidence.

When Napoleon said that the word impossible was found only in the dictionary of fools, he was not mouthing a mere platitude, he was giving expression to what goes by the name of splendid self-confidence.

People who find life unbearable and boring, often fail and blunder. They find it difficult to take any lead. They should examine their own mental picture of themselves that they have nursed for years, and compare it with what they actually are in life. They will find that the two really correspond with each other. In other words, what you are from inside, you show it outside. For example, you may be good, capable, impressive and successful. This is not a chance. It means you have carved your mind accordingly. If you are bad, incapable, unimpressive and unsuccessful, you have moulded your mind in that frame.

The secret of successful living lies in your own vision of yourself, not what others think of you. Or you of them.

If you want to be outgoing, confident, capable of bracing career and life, look to your own thought life. Change your thinking and stick to it. Negativity is the

Importance of Self-Confidence

nightmare of many young people. You may have big aspiration for success but your efforts and thinking are hedged with 'ifs' and 'buts'. You cannot organize yourself nor give proper perspective to a long-range panoramic view. Your confidence is thus crippled. You naturally has a stalemate in your mind. "I am good but there is something fake in me. I think I should end it all." And you does give up. Lack of confidence gets the better of him.

This negativity often shows in depressive moods. A person is locked in himself. He is empty. He feels foul and chained. He is a goner! You feel beaten before you start something new. you either don't try at all or begin half-heartedly, expecting failure.

This attitude invites the failure that is feared. Try to put aside the fear and take a chance. Break the chain of discouraging defeats which seem to prove your inadequacy. Give yourself an opportunity to prove that you can achieve reasonable success. You often say or do the wrong thing.

Your awkwardness comes from a foregone conclusion that you will be awkward. Instead of brooding over the bad impression you expect to make, plan to be cool and tactful. When you study a new subject or try to master a new skill, you keep your mind on how hard it is, how long it will take, and how little you will remember. If you give half of your energy to your work and half to worry about your work, you will be fifty per cent efficient. Keep your mind on the work itself. This is a question of directing attention properly.

Even if you do a job well, you worry because it isn't perfect. If you get eight-five out of a hundred in an examination, you think of the fifteen you didn't get! This is negative. People with great self-doubts are simple perfectionists. They want too much. Acknowledge the fact that a perfect score every time would make you a museum piece instead of a human being. Otherwise, it is true that nothing you ever do will please you. You worry about being too tall, too short, too thin, too heavy, or the shape of some feature.

People who feel inferior should magnify their own faults. Let the problem-solving attitude help. Try to obscure, or compensate for actual physical shortcomings. Remember that the other fellow is usually just as concerned about the impression he makes on you!

If you haven't been to college, or university, you feel bad and take a back seat when others talk. It is not the lack of a diploma—it is the inferiority feeling! Here's another misdirection of attention. Instead of thinking, 'I have no degree', think of the subject under discussion, or the job to be done. If you know, speak up. If you don't know, read up!

You think you don't do as well as your friend. Comparison with those who seem more successful leaves you with no sense of achievement. Do well for yourself! You are a success when you improve on your own record! When something goes badly, you should think it is your own fault. If it rained and spoiled a picnic, you would feel responsible and apologetic. This is negativism at its best. It is confidence-shattering.

Lame excuses must be avoided. But there is such a thing as poor business conditions over which you have little or no control. Self-doubt causes you to absorb troubles and add to your sense of failure. Give them their due! But

Importance of Self-Confidence

not over-due! Do not boast or act high, run everything down, even though you do not really enjoy it. You are acting as a wind-bag. This is compensation game. A person who feels inferior, puffs himself up or pushes other people down. This does not bolster his ego, and it only serves to irritate those he meets. Put up a mental stop-sign when you estimate people and what they do.

Realize that the origin of vanity is in the insecurity feeling of itself. You talk too quickly, answer questions too fast, and greet people with nervous haste. You are undignified. People who doubt on themselves act as if they thought no one would wait for them to speak, and as if it was always they who must snap to attention and say it first.

Again, use that stop-deliberate! sign when with other people. It's a strain at first, but a relief to see that you can slow down and achieve a feeling of stability. You spend a lot of time telling people where they get off—in your imagination. In real life, you rarely express any resentment and let people impose on you too much.

The cure is to find suitable expression in real life. Plan to express yourself firmly and calmly when you find it necessary. It will do you good to find that people soon accept your new image of yourself as a person who stands up for his rights. You cannot be over-ridden. When you have a big task, you think of the whole thing at once. You never feel you have done enough on any one day because there is always so much more to do.

You need a schedule for tackling a big job. Assign a day for each part of your job. Concentrate on one part at a time, in one day. This lets you know when you say, "I've done my day's work!" You envy those with special skills and special funds of knowledge. You think you are not good enough at any one particular thing.

If you are not, then you have never tried to be. Consider your high points. Language? Photography? Music? Some aspect of business? Begin to build one or two of those high points by study and practice.

You put things off till the last minute, then find yourself terribly rushed, do a bad job, and prove again—as you see it—that you are not very good. Postponement always makes a job looks harder. Plan when to do it and at that exact time jump to it, and do it. No procrastination.

When people criticize you, it makes you feel simply terrible for a long time. People who doubt themselves tend to dangle by the opinions of others. They lack stability.

Sometimes a critic is trying to make you feel low and make himself feel more secure. In that case, feel sorry for him. You have accepted yourself as an inferior person, who will play an inferior role in life. There's a world of difference between being inferior and feeling inferior. Yet, a person who feels inferior for years often comes to think he is inferior. Remember, you can change the role you play in life with proper effort.

Take a few moments every evening to note exactly how inferiority attitudes have caused trouble. Plan to handle similar situations more effectively. Don't expect to "snap out of it" overnight. Gradual improvement should cause you to congratulate yourself. It is satisfaction from reasonable progress that builds confidence.

■■■

Census 2011

Census 2011 or the 15th Indian National Census was conducted in two phases, which included house listing and population enumeration. April 1, 2010 marked the start of house listing phase. It involved collection of information about all buildings. Information for National Population Register was also collected in the first phase, which will be used to issue a 12-digit unique identification number to all Indians by Unique Identification Authority of India.

The second population enumeration phase was conducted between 9 to 28 February 2011. Census has been conducted in India since 1872 and 2011 marks the first time biometric information was collected. According to the provisional reports released on March 31, 2011, the Indian population increased to 1.21 billion with a decadal growth of 17.64%. Adult literacy rate has increased to 74.04% with a decadal growth of 9.21%.

Over 2.7 million officials visited households in about 7,000 towns and 600,000 villages, classifying the population according to gender, religion, education and occupation. The cost of the exercise was in the region of 22bn rupees ($490m; £300m). The exercise, conducted every 10 years, faced big challenges, not least India's vast area and diversity of cultures and opposition from the manpower is involved.

Information on castes was included in the census following demands from several ruling coalition leaders including Lalu Prasad Yadav, Sharad Yadav and Mulayam

Singh Yadav supported by opposition parties Bharatiya Janata Party, Akali Dal, Shiv Sena and Anna Dravida Munnetra Kazhagam. Information on caste was last collected during British Raj in 1931. During the early census, people often exaggerated their caste status to garner social status and it is expected that people downgrade it now in the expectation of gaining government benefits.

The population of India at 0:00 hours of 1 March 2011 was 1,210,193,422. India added 181 million to its population since 2001, slightly lower than the population of Brazil. India with 2.4% of the world's surface area accounts for 17.5% of its population. Uttar Pradesh is the most populous state with roughly 200 million people. A little more than 6 out of every 10 Indians live in Uttar Pradesh, Maharashtra, Bihar, West Bengal, Madhya Pradesh and Tamil Nadu.

■ ■ ■

Technology—Bane or Boon?

The overt observation of some knowledgeable persons who passionately feel concerned for the welfare of humanity, in the wake of scientific strides and technological triumphs, laments that "technology creates more problems than it solves".

Their concern echoes the similar sentiments of thinkers like J.G.Ballard for whom, "technology dictates the languages in which we speak and think.

Either we use those languages or we remain mute", and for Omar Bradley "our technology has already outstripped our ability to control it".

Despite these jarring notes, technology has acquired a halo that is almost impossible to shake off.

Who can deny the robust role and range of technology that we experience in our every day life. If we care to look at the scintillating side of technology, we find space technology and its applications provide useful data for natural disaster monitoring, solving environment problems, improve telecommunications and provide other basic services.

Through fax, e-mail and the Internet, information technology has outstripped all barriers that time and space had placed in man's search for instant information. Though electronic information is hard to control, yet the individual newsgatherer is visible and vulnerable. The latest in the success story is the likely boom that bio-technology promises to unfold in the years to come.

Rightly, biotechnology is being seen by scientists and entrepreneurs alike as the next big thing with the potential to revolutionise the fields of agriculture, health and medicine.

The promises are many: disease-resistant and high-yield crops that could solve the world's food problems; new medicines and drug delivery systems to cure diseases and prevent genetically inherited disorders; and new enzymes that make industrial production more efficient and cost-effective.

For ages the axiom, nothing is good or bad but thinking makes it so, was the golden rule that moulded human perceptions and concrete actions.

With the advent of science and technology, and their subsequent sway over human ideas, intuitions and ideologies, it is now 'the use or abuse' of technology that renders it either 'a blessing or a bane' for humanity that lives and survives on the ever- spreading tentacles of technology.

In short, it is the technology that rules the roost now and keeps its ambience alive all the time in various manifestations. With the frontiers of technology influencing all aspects of life, both in terms of time and space, it is anybody's guess as to what the future holds in store for humanity, that has become so enamoured of technology.

If the past is any guide, one can learn a lot from the happenings of the 20th century, that used and abused scientific and technological achievements for increasing physical comforts and living standards, fighting the two world wars, resorting to nuclear bombing, land mines and other means of mass deaths and destruction, dislocation of millions resulting in untold miseries and sufferings.

In the face of so much good that we expect from science and technology, scientists warn that if we do not change our ways, our civilization is not likely to survive.

Man's greed, aided and abetted by science and technology, have already over-exploited and abused the earth's material resources and destroyed its ecosystems.

Forests are vanishing and there is increased desertification, the seas and oceans are stained with death because of the poisons that we have poured into them.

We have even polluted the rain with poisonous smoke from our industrial chimneys. We have not only raped the soil and denigrated the ecosystems, but also lost touch with our inner-self.

There is no denying that our cares and concerns are being controlled by technology, in its various forms and facets.

Whether in company or in solitude, technology has come to occupy a pivotal place in our day-to-day life. If the despots use it to perpetuate their repressive rule, the terrorists have employed it to explode symbols of progress.

With no end to man's rapacious nature in sight, technology has become a hand-maiden of unscrupulous exploiters of natural resources and immoral traders of wild life species.

Technology as it reigns supreme over our intellect and imagination, is redefining human relations. In a bid to hit the jackpot, or make a quick buck, the individual has lost his identity and, in the bargain, has fallen an easy prey to alienation and estrangement.

Smarting under physical fatigue and mental stress, he has become a victim of the phenomenon of being an "outsider" among his own people.

Despite a host of benefits that technology has conferred on us in varying degrees, the onslaught of anger and angst is very much conspicuous. If today we are scared of some impending disaster, it is because technology has given such powers to individuals and groups which even the demons or deities of mythology did not enjoy.

We are standing at the threshold where technology as a source of boon or brazenness is staring in our face. In moments of introspection, we must bear in mind what Aldous Huxley had said: "Technological progress has merely provided us with more efficient means for going backwards".

■■■

Economic Reforms in India

The economic reforms or liberalization in India mark a shift from socialist economy to a market economy. Initiated by the late Prime Minister of India, Shri P.V. Narasimha Rao and his Finance Minister Manmohan Singh, their immediate cause was a foreign exchange crisis during Chandrashekhar government when India had to sell its gold reserves.

Reforms ended the Licence Raj (investment, industrial and import licensing) and several public monopolies.

The United Front government brought a budget that encouraged reforms but the 1997 Asian financial meltdown and political instability caused economic stagnation.

The Vajpayee administration continued with privatization, reduced taxes, introduced a firm fiscal policy aimed at lessening deficits and debts and enhanced initiatives for public works.

India under Nehru and Congress followed the Soviet model of planned economy to rid India of the exploitive colonial British economic policy and its vestiges after independence.

Five-Year Plans achieved much but also led to heavy centralization, inefficient State capitalism, State monopolies in mining, machine tools, water, telecommunications, insurance, and electrical plants.

The so-called Hindu rate of growth became a joke as India stagnated at 3.5% from 1950s to 1980s, while per capita income averaged at 1.3%, even as Pakistan grew by 8%, Indonesia by 9%, Thailand by 9%, South Korea by 10% and Taiwan by 12%.

Today, the private sector has become an active participant in the telecommunications sector. Insurance has been opened to private investors, both domestic and foreign.

The economy has grown at more than 6 per cent, coupled with full macroeconomic stability. The rate of inflation is once again coming down after spiralling alarm.

Rising incomes have helped reduce poverty. According to official figures, the proportion of poor in total population had declined from 40 per cent in 1993-1994 to 26 per cent in 2000.

Most importantly, the attitude toward reforms has changed. Virtually every political party today recognizes the need for continued reforms.

Though slow pace of reforms is credited with India's firm fundamentals and weathering the shock of global economic depression, yet all is not well with India's reforms and the fiscal deficit remains in doldrums.

The combined deficit at the Centre and States exceeds 10 per cent of GDP. This deficit is unsustainable; it is also crowding out private investment.

Infrastructure like roads, railways and ports all need expansion. Improvement in quality of service and delivery systems is a must.

The government has recently started building roads, but the pace remains slow. India's power sector is also in a horrible State.

Economic reforms have bypassed agriculture. Farmers are committing suicide and do not get full market price for their product.

Procurement prices are below the market price. Further, export restrictions must be phased out.

If India grows at 6 per cent per annum on a sustained basis, it will take 14 years to reach the current level of per capita income of People's Republic of China, 36 years to reach Thailand's, and 104 years to reach that of the United States.

Thus, the need for accelerated growth can hardly be overemphasized.

■ ■ ■

Successful Versus Effective Leader

A leader is anyone who influences a group toward obtaining a particular result. Leadership is not dependent on title or formal authority. Political examples are Gandhi and Jai Prakash Narayan.

An individual who is appointed to a supreme position has the right to command and enforce obedience by virtue of the authority of his or her position. Mrs Indira Gandhi was, thus, an effective leader as Prime Minister.

According to some experts, the influence of leaders on organizational outcomes is overrated and romanticized and this results into biased attributions about leaders.

Still, it is largely accepted that leadership is central to a performing organization and leaders do contribute to key organizational outcomes.

In order to facilitate successful performance it is important to understand and accurately measure leadership performance.

It is important to distinguish between performance and effectiveness. Performance reflects behaviour, while effectiveness implies the assessment of actual organizational outcomes.

So, it becomes important to delineate the particular behaviours that contribute to key organizational outcomes versus the actual organizational outcomes.

At times, outcomes may be subject to external factors and beyond the control of the leader and it may not be easy to determine what exactly is driving a particular outcome.

'Leadership effectiveness refers to the ability to influence others and achieve collective goals', according to Judge, Bono, Ilies, and Gerhardt study.

Some researchers, however, suggest that leadership success ought to be based on the effectiveness of the team, group, or organization.

But, leadership effectiveness is "often based on the perceptions of subordinates, peers, or supervisors.

Many studies rely on peer rankings on who emerges as a leader in a given situation, even though many personality traits have been associated with leadership emergence.

For example, extraversion and openness to experience have been positively associated with leader effectiveness, while neuroticism is negatively related to leader effectiveness.

The relationship between personality traits and performance outcomes is stronger for leader emergence than for leader effectiveness. Another related concept is leadership advancement over a long career span.

Early longitudinal research had suggested that factors such as interpersonal, cognitive, and administrative skills were related to leader advancement.

While overlap exists among these constructs, some distinction has to be made between job performance and effectiveness of leadership.

By Job performance is meant contributions of the leader to organizational goal accomplishment. Job effectiveness refers to evaluation of the results achieved by the leader.

Effectiveness can be influenced by a variety of external factors, outside of the leader's immediate control.

As such, it may not be accurate to attribute all the achievement factors to an individual's leadership capabilities. For example, so many CEO's became achievers only during the booming spree.

Therefore, while assessing performance, it is appropriate to examine elements within the leader's control, such as specific behaviours that facilitate collective action and goal achievement.

Evaluating leadership in such a manner is necessary for more accurately identifying predictors of leader performance.

Likewise, analysts should carefully weigh leadership behaviours in order to more clearly establish the importance of leadership to organisational outcomes.

■■■

The Role of a Manager in an Organization

A manager in an organization is not always a leader. Management and leadership are two different concepts, though often appear to overlap.

Modern organizations tend to be complex and operate in a global business environment. Therefore, there is renewed focus on the importance of management and leadership and their distinctive roles in promoting and advancing the interests of the organization. Hard competition and continuous pressures for change, demand that managers and leaders work closely together for achieving business goals. On the practical level, a manager is called upon to evince the quality of leadership and a leader the knack for managing difficult situations in their respective roles in any organization. Pragmatically speaking, the distinction between a manager and leader is not problematic. "A manager is often portrayed as a procedural administrator/supervisor—an individual in an organization with recognized formal authority who plans, coordinates and implements the existing directions of the organization." A leader, on the other hand, is defined as someone who occupies a position of influence within a group that "extends beyond supervisory responsibility and formal authority" and is involved in devising new directions and leading followers "to attain group, organizational and societal goals". This distinction between the supervisory manager and visionary leader has to be understood in terms of their respective tasks and functions.

Dunsford, a management guru, believes that management is concerned with 'efficiency'—with tasks such as coordinating resources and implementing policy, while leadership has to concern itself with 'effectiveness' of making decisions, setting directions and principles, formulating issues and grappling with problems. Katz, however, has identified three critical managerial skills and the last two happen to be attributes of competent leadership. These are: technical skills (the ability to perform particular tasks or activities); interpersonal skills (the ability to work well with other people); and conceptual skills (the ability to see the 'big picture').

Modern leadership theory supports an integrated approach to management and leadership. Early work on leadership identified the various styles of leadership based on personal traits and behaviour of an effective leader, such as drive, desire to lead, decisiveness, honesty and integrity, self-confidence, intelligence and job relevant knowledge. The behaviourist models focus on the relationship between a leader's actions and their impact on the attitudes and performance of employees. These studies compared various styles of leadership, such as authoritarian and democratic styles. They are studied if an effective leader is more prone to an efficient accomplishment of a task rather than being inclined to the welfare of employees and subordinates.

The traditional distinction between a manager and a leader is disappearing. Modern business operates in the midst of uncertainties as the current global slowdown and enveloping financial crisis show. Accordingly, the role of a manager demands flexibility, dynamism, management skills as well as leadership quality.

■■■

The Tasks of a Leader

There are several ways of defining a leader. The one who leads others is a simple and complete definition. But, then, what are the tasks of a leader? Leadership is a much sought after quality and every organization needs good and effective leaders to lead the organization to success and for the achievement of its goals.

Some persons are born leaders, for others leadership gets thrust upon. In a given organization, the Head of the Organization or the Chief Executive Officer is accepted as a leader irrespective of his or her possessing the quality of leadership.

Management Gurus, more or less, agree on the following tasks for the leader of any organization, irrespective of its nature and goals: A leader must be able to:

1. Impart vision and direction to her/his organization
2. Affirm and articulate values that she/he cherishes for her/his organization
3. Set high standards of performance and raise the level of expectations
4. She/he must make herself/himself accountable
5. Must be able to motivate others within the organization
6. Achieve unity in the organization
7. Involve others in decision-making

    The leader's most important task is to clarify the overall goals of the organization. This is what transform a mere crowd into a community, and a directionless mob into a group with a purpose. A crowd in a fair, for instance, is joyous, free spirited but selfoccupied. In the same way, a gathering may have individually talented and even highly motivated people but they will achieve nothing if they lack vision or goal to achieve collectively.

The success of leadership depends on personal characteristics that include experience, imagination, persuasiveness, farsightedness, and astuteness in interpersonal dealings.

The leader will not be able take his/her organization very far if he is not able to generate, manage and monitor the use of resources.

Most organizations have resources available, but seldom are they sufficient for everything that everyone wants to do. Resources do not manage themselves; allocation and monitoring systems have to be established. Budget, timetables, staffing plans, policies, procedures and priorities need to be set and worked out.

Empowerment and delegation of authority demands astute handling because human material is not like machines or furniture that can be allocated in a fixed pattern.

To select, develop, and share power with subordinates/associates is an art that is not easy to learn or acquire.

Winning trust and loyalty of disparate persons can be demanding but are necessary for the task of assigning tasks to others. Decision-making and responsibility need to be dispersed for accomplishing current tasks and preparing others for future leadership. Relations within and outside an organization play an important role and this is yet another essential task for a leader.

Building relations and range of contacts require friendliness, wit, wisdom, negotiation skills, and the ability to entertain or at least to hold the attention of a wide range of people.

A leader also has to be Enterprising because finding new opportunities and creating desirable change are also his/her task. Every organization has certain momentum that imparts its continuity yet, obsolescence is a constant challenge for a leader.

In large organizations this can require a massive refocusing of people and resources. Leaders are needed at all levels but most people would want to follow rather than lead. Finally, a great leader creates more leaders, Like Gandhi.

■ ■ ■

Management: Its Nature and Scope

Management studies are of recent origin but management is as old as man's need for organizing work and activities. Management now has become a 'discipline'.

Numerous Management Gurus have emerged. They have been defining, redefining and commenting on the scope and nature of Management.

Question as to whether Management is a Science or an Art has been resolved by saying that Management is the "oldest of the arts and youngest of the sciences".

Management is different from other higher studies because of its inclusive nature. It, not only deals with the theory and practice of production of goods and services but also with development and deployment of human resources.

Manufacturing, procuring, distributing and delivering of goods in a competitive environment and international markets demand efficient and effective operations.

Selling, promoting and marketing of goods too call for coordinated efforts and innovative ideas. Services to customers and the analysis of queue systems are yet another aspect of Management.

Historically, Management Studies have their origin in the body of knowledge stemming from industrial engineering.

This body of knowledge formed the basis of the first MBA programme, and has become "central to operations management as used across diverse business sectors, industry, consulting and non-profit organizations".

It is not only the scope but also the nature of Management that demands proper understanding. How the various "parts" of an organization relate to their "whole" and what contribution they make to its efficient and productive working are important issues.

(Looked at from these considerations) an organization needs to devise standards for measuring its performance. Here, the distinction between efficiency and effectiveness assumes significance.

Often, Management is divided into Operations management and Production management. Operations management is the process whereby resources or inputs are converted into more useful products.

Thus, there appears hardly any difference between "production management and operations management".

However, "production management" is used for a system that produces tangible goods. Operations management is used for a system that transforms various inputs into tangible services, for example, banks, airlines, utilities, pollution control agencies, super bazaars, educational institutions, libraries, consultancy firms and police departments, and, of course, manufacturing enterprises.

The second distinction relates to the evolution of the subject. 'Operations management' is currently in vogue. Earlier, 'Production management' was in use. Both terms are interchangeably used.

Stanley Vance has defined Management as simply the

process of decision-making and control over actions of human beings for the attainment of pre-determined goals. Lawrence Appley says it is the "accomplishment results" through others.

According to John Mee, management is the art of maximizing results and minimizing efforts for securing maximum happiness and prosperity for the employees and the employer and giving the public best possible service. The scope as well as nature of Management, thus, remains undefined but its goals are hotly pursued.

■■■

What is Wrong with Child Labour?

Not all work is bad for children. According to social scientists most kinds of work are unobjectionable, if they are not exploitative. School boys delivering newspapers is a common sight in the developed countries. This activity benefits the child as he learns how to work, gain responsibility, and earn some pocket money. But if the child is not paid, the same work becomes exploitative.

The United Nations Children Fund (UNICEF)'s 1997 State of the World's Children Report says: "Children's work needs to be seen as happening along a continuum, with destructive or exploitative work at one end and beneficial work—promoting or enhancing children's development without interfering with their schooling, recreation and rest—at the other.

And between these two poles are vast areas of work that need not negatively affect a child's development. Social scientists agree but draw the line between acceptable and unacceptable work differently.

International conventions define children as aged 18 and under. Individual governments may define "child" according to different ages or other criteria. "Child" and "childhood" are also defined differently by different cultures.

In fact, children's abilities and maturity vary widely and, therefore, defining a child's maturity by calendar age can be misleading.

In 2000, the ILO estimated, "246 million child workers

aged 5 to 17 were involved in child labour, of which 171 million were involved in work that by its nature is hazardous to their safety, physical or mental health, and moral development.

Moreover, some 8.4 million children were engaged in so-called 'unconditional' or worst forms of child labour, such as forced and bonded labour, conscription by military forces in armed conflict, trafficking, commercial, sexual and other forms of exploitation. In India, child labour is exploitative in the extreme.

Growing children are employed as domestic help and live in miserable conditions. They are paid low and sleep in staircases or on the road.

Those employed by the roadside *dhabas* or teashops in the cities or on the highways likewise lead a life of deprivation and dreariness.

Yet, if they do not take up this type of work, they face starvation and ill-treatment at home, even at the hands of parents and relatives. There are laws prohibiting child labour but in India the laws are seldom implemented.

More boys than girls work outside their homes. Increasingly, however, more girls are working in some jobs: for instance, as domestic maids. Being a maid in someone's house is risky.

Cut off from friends and family, these little maids can easily be physically or sexually abused by their employers and even by neighbours or unknown visitors. Children in hazardous and dangerous jobs are in danger of injury and death.

According to UNICEF, it is a myth that

1. "Child labour is only a problem in developing countries. ... children routinely work in all industrialised countries, and hazardous forms of child labour can be found in many countries.
2. Child labour will only disappear when poverty disappears.
3. Only a very small proportion of all child workers are employed in export industries—probably less than 5 per cent. Most of the world's child labourers are actually found in the informal sector—selling on the street, at work in agriculture or hidden away in houses—far from the reach of official labour inspectors and from media scrutiny."

In our view, poverty is largely responsible for what is wrong with child labour; other causes are not as pervasive.

■ ■ ■

Tradition and Modernity: Friends or Foes?

Jean Baudrillard, a major theoretician of the European present, characterizes the present state of affairs, at least in the Western context, as "after the orgy": the "orgy", according to him, was the moment when modernity exploded upon us, the moment of liberation in every sphere—political liberation, sexual liberation, liberation of the forces of production, liberation of the forces of destruction, women's liberation, liberation of unconscious drives liberation of art. It was an orgy of the real, the rational, of criticism and anti-criticism, of development and of the crisis of development.

There has been now an over-production of objects, signs, messages, ideologies and satisfactions. When everything has been liberated, one can only simulate (reproduce) liberation, simulate the orgy, pretending to carry on in the same direction; accelerating without knowing we are accelerating in a void.

The impact of technology is fast changing our everyday life too: the major difference may be that we are not in the age "after the orgy", for, our revolutions have not succeeded, but have aborted, got stopped in the midway, our utopia has taken an atavistic (reappearance of characteristic or quality not seen for many generations) turn, our Janus now has both its faces turned towards the past. Our struggles for emancipation—social, sexual, aesthetic—seem to have left us half-way, have failed to bring about a transformation that embraces all the layers of society.

Nevertheless, tradition gives a sense of identity. There is an element of security in it; yet innovation is necessary to prevent stagnation and rot. Society must and will continue to innovate. Cultural exchange is the stuff out of which social processes are made.

Traditional medicine, for example, was humane and modern medicine is merciless; traditional science had built in correctives, but modern science and technology is aggressively domineering; in tradition there was respect for plurality, but modern societies are self-consciously homogenising. Modern societies may breed fascists, but traditional ones had their share of Changez Khans too.

True, modernity has got many emancipatory possibilities. But then, modernity is not free from its discontent—dislocation of the individual from the protective context of family-kinship ties, alienation from the communitarian ideal and loss of collective memory.

Perhaps, in matters of faith and fashions, it is neither the hard stands taken by both, nor the rigidity of their arguments that brings them nearer to each other. Just as all that meets the eye may not be the only reality, in the same vein, to assert with authority that tradition and modernity are incompatible is to rush in where even the angels would pause and ponder to tread.

Seemingly, both tradition and modernization look to be at loggerheads with each other, but on deeper analysis, one finds that even the most traditional/orthodox societies have prepared themselves, though reluctantly, to accept new realities which modernity has unfolded with an unprecedented speed. It is almost hypocritical to disown the advantages of modernization in our daily perceptions and practices.

Since no age or generation is fully static in thought and action, there are always some prudent persons who take on the untenable and anachronistic spell of traditions and prefer new ideas and concepts (that) are born out of the existing realities.

For analytical/inquisitive minds, tradition is stagnant in nature and nuance and modernization is consistent with change and challenge of times. If some knowledgeable persons opine that tradition and modernity are not friends, they are not much off the mark. To them tradition is a morass of beliefs and customs that refuse to liberate human minds from its stranglehold.

On the contrary, modernisation is a process that tries to update men, minds and machines.

Since the trio holds key to all material progress and prosperity, it is not unnatural that both tradition and modernity should live in a 'love-hate' relationship with each other.

■ ■ ■

Promotion of Sports: A Social Necessity

The importance of sports and games is being increasingly recognised in India from both the educational and social points of view. More and more funds are being allocated for encouraging sports in schools, colleges and universities; in fact, sports have become an essential part of the curricula. Time was when only a few students who were fond of certain games, like hockey, football, cricket or tennis, were allowed special facilities.

But now regular programmes are drawn up in all educational institutions to persuade as many students as possible, regardless of special aptitudes, to participate in games and not merely watch matches occasionally to cheer up their favourite teams and attend the prize distribution functions at the end of a sports season. Educationalists and others have come to the conclusion that it is in the interest of society as a whole that adequate facilities should be provided, depending of course upon the availability of funds, for games and sports for the country's youth, both boys and girls. Sports foster friendship and amity.

Nor does the belief hold good any more that those who take part in sports or games would be no good at studies and that each year their absence from the class or shortage of lectures would be condoned because they can either attend to their studies or be on the playing field for some game or the other. It is felt that apart from some exceptional cases of students showing their extraordinary talent and skill in certain games, or students who are expected to be high on the merit list in university examinations, most other students should play one game or other, not necessarily for achieving distinctions but for the sake of sport.

Several factors need to be taken into account in this connection. First, physical fitness is of the utmost importance for everyone, young and old. Participation in games and sports invariably ensures good health, fitness and, generally, freedom from ailments of various types which find easy victims among people who take no physical exercise and are either lazy, indolent or desk-bound or are book worms and keep studying all the time under the mistaken concept that they can win success in life by studying all the time and concentrating on the development of their mental faculties. They feel convinced that brain matters, not brawn and that spending hours on the play-field is a waste of time. But such students, sooner or later, find that unless the human body is kept in smooth trim and in an overall fit condition, even then brain will refuse to co-operate after some time. Actually, physical fitness is essential for proficiency in studies and for winning distinctions in examinations. Ailing bodies do not make for sharp brains. Exercise in some form or another is necessary, and sports provide an easy method to ensure such fitness.

Secondly, regular participation in sports provides a healthy channel for diversion of energies. Wherever students and other youth participate in sports regularly ensure constructive sublimation, misdirection of youthful vigour is much less and the tendency to indulge in indiscipline, mischiefs and disruptive activities of various kinds is curbed. Young people have surplus energy, and if this is fruitfully utilised, the foundations are laid for a healthy society where people are fully aware of the need for discipline, co-operative effort, team spirit, the cult of sportsmanship, of joint devotion to the achievement of a common goal in collaboration with others. They also learn to cultivate the vital quality of learning how to work together, to become not only good winners but also good losers. Both sides playing a game cannot win simultaneously and ups and downs are common. The losers must learn to take their defeat sportingly. The right spirit can be learnt on the playgrounds. There is no point in bearing a grudge against the rivals; today's losers can be tomorrow's winners, as in society in general and in political arena in particular.

Thirdly, the statement that "the battle of Waterloo was won on the play-fields of Eton", implying that playing games and the spirit of sportsmanship help to inculcate lasting values which make for good soldiers, good fighters and good discipline, apart from promoting 100 per cent physical fitness. While most people concede the importance of sports in a healthy society and under a good government, there has also been much criticism, which is fully justified, too, about the craze, enthusiasm and fervour displayed by people of all ages, especially the country's youth (except the sober elders and duty-conscious officers and employees), whenever cricket Test matches are being played in India or abroad and wherever India is one of the participants. Work virtually comes to a stop in offices, factories, schools and colleges. Everyone starts listening to cricket commentaries, forget their work and duty, in effect lose themselves mentally in the process; all their attention is concentrated on the ball-by-ball Test commentaries. At wayside shops, in trains and buses, on ships and in aircraft, it is the same story during the cricket season—people attentively listening to radio commentaries or watching the cricket matches on TV. Surely this is not what we mean by a sport and sportsmanship. The right description for this habit is "craze". It does not develop any of the values which sports and games inculcate—discipline and playing the game in the right spirit. Tennis, hockey and football are more vigorous games, and a match is over in about an hour. Watching such games is understandable and should be encouraged but cricket Test matches last for five or six days each, and the waste of time of the general public who listen to the commentaries from morning to late afternoon can be well imagined.

Some observers have contended that there is a close link between sports, a country's industrial development and the general progress of the society. That is why it is contended, most of the gold medals at the Olympics are bagged by advanced countries such as the USA, Russia, Germany, France and Britain too manages to bag few of them. Of the eastern countries, China and Japan plunder most of the gold and silver medals. Is there also a link between the performance in sports and a country's military might? Militarily China is the most powerful country in the East, but Japan, which matches the USA in industrial, especially in electronic and advancement, does well in sports despite of its small size. India is a large country of continental size, and having the proper incentives and the necessary facilities, this country's sportsmen should do well on the sports field, but whether it is the climatic factor, the lack of adequate nutrition and of incentives, our sportsmen do not compare favourably with those of the USA, Russia, Germany and Australia.

In any case, the relatively poor show of our athletes in international competitions does not weaken the case of encouraging sports which help to lay the foundations of a healthy sound society. The cost is returned in several-fold.

■ ■ ■

Fast Life: Thrill or Thorn?

The present-day trends and tendencies on the part of individuals and nations hold the view that 'speed and success' are synonymous both in content and context. Opinions may differ among knowledgeable persons on the subject of 'fast life, fast buck and fast food'. For some the hectic pace of life is heading towards a priceless possession, whereas for some it is a dubious drift towards perils or problems. Polemics apart, like nations, individuals too have to grasp the basic or rigorous reality that we live in a highly competitive world in which the rise or decline of individuals is determined by the rapid pace of speed with which they respond to new challenges and constantly changing circumstances. The ability to keep pace with the mobility and momentum of fast moving times, is also the determination to sweep aside odds and obstacles and press ahead with reform and restructurings and is also the key to success.

"Necessity is the mother of invention." If today, the requirements of combating forces inimical to progress and prosperity are urgent and pressing, so is the urgency to accelerate the tempo of our concepts and concrete actions. It is due to the rapid pace of life and other compulsions that we are obliged to win the race against time and adopt all possible means to rush help to those peoples who are in dire straits. Since there is no gain without pain, it is but natural that the more we exert to break previous records and accomplish targets, the more we suffer the ill effects of our burnt out energies.

It is not only individuals who have benefited the most from rapid strides made on the path-breaking parameters of 'speed and success', but the world as a whole has achieved the unprecedented supremacy over 'time and space'. The speed with which we can travel across the globe, and even probe space and other planets, is a telling tribute to the tone and temper of life that has adjusted itself so well with mind-boggling miracles brought about by 'man, mind and machine'.

Undoubtedly, speed offers thrill. The axiom 'slow and steady wins the race' has lost much of its relevance. The need of the hour is to steal a march over others, be the natural phenomena or human hindrances, and register success stories without delay. There is no denying face that rapid pace of life has contributed a lot to progress and prosperity (that we see around) in patches and pouches.

No other era stands out for its conspicuous contradictions and palpable paradoxes as ours. If there are path-breaking success stories, fully backed by race against time, there are innumerable instances of anger, angst and alienation staring us at the face. We are living in the best of times, as also in the worst of times. We are a living witness to enthralling, enchanting, delicious, delectable paradoxical ironies and ironical paradoxes.

'Sky is the limit' has become both a motive and a marvel. Passions and pursuits are directed toward tackling many problems that confronts us. The state of helplessness in the face of colossal upheavals is a thing of the past. Targets and deadlines no longer pose serious challenges, because human beings, with their hearts in 'proper place' and minds in 'meticulous mould', have learnt to outsmart or outwit them.

To say or assert with an authority that the spectrum of life is all colourful and there are no dark spots, is only half-true. The other half is littered with the fearsome findings of psychiatrists and psychologists, who see the emerging trends among the most successful and busy bodies highly disturbing. A thrill in senses and a thorn in flesh—this is how one can describe the curves and contours of the rapid pace of present-day life.

Given the pressure of the work place and stiff deadlines and targets, health is not a priority at this level. Spondylitis, high blood pressure, backache and ulcers that are directly related to stress, even a niggling cardiac problem, are worries that today's baby boomers are grappling with. No doubt, the rewards offered for good work have gone up. So there is an urge to outperform others. There is certainly a trend for people who are at the top and financially comfortable to venture out into other unrelated areas, which they had missed out because of their hectic life style. There is a massive trend and is visible more and more. The lament:

'What is this life if, full of care,

We have no time to stand and stare.'

—W.H. Davies

is both timely and telling.

■ ■ ■

Prosperity Through Environment

Protection of the environment in all its forms has been receiving much public attention at domestic and international forums. The question is by no means new but it has acquired much greater urgency than ever before because of the ceaseless pollution of the atmosphere, the reckless destruction of the multi-faceted gifts of Nature by thoughtless human beings.

Among the offenders are people who are, or should be, aware of the folly of their deeds and the irreparable damages they are doing to the safety and prosperity of mankind, the present and the future generations. Hence the environmentalists' clarion call.

Human existence depends upon the environment. Few persons would now question the statement that we have been poisoning or destroying valuable resources on earth (including water) and also in the air—all in the name of economic development.

In fact, development, expansion and growth are the key slogans in the modern world; nothing else seems to matter. Senseless poisoning is proceeding with unbelievable speed. While genocide rightly receives severe condemnation, "ecoside"—ruthless murder of the environment—has only recently become a cognisable offence.

After all, it is the biosphere, that is, the air and water encasing the earth, besides the green cover and the wildlife, that sustain life on this planet. In chemical terms, it is the mixture and fine balance of oxygen, nitrogen, carbon dioxide and water vapour that is vital for life. These are operated and maintained by multiple biological processes. For centuries, man took for granted that the bounties of Nature were inexhaustible and that the resources got renewed automatically. Both these assumptions have lately been proved wrong.

The struggle now is for adequate renewal of such resources as man has to use every day, and also for the preservation and protection of as many resources as possible.

Attempts are being made to check the reckless destruction of precious environment. Scientists have warned that mankind might have to return to the much-dreaded "ice age" if the reckless destruction of trees, other greenery and natural resources continues at the pace associated with "modern" progress, especially in industry.

A look-back in this regard would be helpful. Oddly enough, it was only in 1972 that the first systematic international effort was made to take stock of the situation and plan adequate steps to counter the process of destruction.

The step was the UN Conference on Environment held in Sweden. The conference was poorly attended, for political and other reasons.

Then came the UN Habitat Conference on Human Settlements in 1975 in Vancouver and the UN Desertification Conference in Nairobi in 1977 to check the ruinous growth of deserts.

But in many ways the year 1990 marked a specific advance in the programmes for saving mankind from disaster. The occasion marked recognition of the basic fact that the environmentalists are fighting for the concept of sustainable progress with the belief that environment and development are not opposite poles. In this connection, the observation of the Brundtland Commission (in its report published in 1987) was recalled.

The Commission said: "Economy is not just about the production of wealth, and ecology is not just about the protection of Nature; they are both equally relevant for improving the lot of mankind."

The Montreal Protocol was very much in the news in 1990. The aim of the Protocol is to save the precious ozone layer from chemical damage.

All enlightened countries now concede that the destruction of the ozone layer will have serious consequences on human, animal and plant life.

There is no denying that the major culprits in causing pollution and damaging the ozone layer are the developed countries.

These countries have been gaining all through the years by using cheap CFCs and have harmed the global environment. If they want the developing countries to restrain themselves from following the same course, they should assist them.

Though the developing countries produce only a small proportion of the world output of CFCs, they require massive assistance to switch over to new technologies and to less harmful substitutes. Therefore, a large fund is needed.

The Government of India's growing concern over this

problem is obvious from the establishment of a department and Ministry for Environment and the series of laws passed to check the practices that endanger the environment. These are: The Air (Prevention and Control of Pollution) Act, 1981, the Water (Pollution and Control of Pollution) Act, 1974, the Environment (Protection) Act, May 1986, the Forests (Conservation) Act, 1980, the Wildlife Protection Act, 1972, which has been frequently amended to make it more effective. Besides, there is a full-fledged national forest policy, several programmes and projects to conserve the environment and check the destructive practices.

There have been many social conflicts over the issue of natural resources in India. The controversies over the Sardar Sarovar Dam and the Narmada Projects are among the outstanding examples. Competing claims and Inter-State disputes over water and forests are quite common.

As in the case of land disputes, the controversies over the natural resources involve vested interests. There are, in many cases, unequal antagonists; several agrarian conflicts have ecological roots. The grave consequences of some of the dam construction projects have been highlighted by the numerous agitations carried on by voluntary agencies and courageous individuals.

The Chipko movement started by the brave Sunderlal Bahuguna to save the Garhwal forests won well-deserved international recognition.

The social good has to be weighed against an individual benefit and a rational balance needs to be struck. The writing on the wall is clear. If the present generation fails to preserve and protect Nature's bounty, the coming generations will hold us guilty of betraying an invaluable trust.

But in their excessive zeal, the environmentalists ignore a vital aspect. India needs more foodgrains, more water, more electricity, more industries for manufacturing and finishing goods for domestic consumption and exports—all for the social good.

Dams over rivers and construction of large power houses to harness energy sources enable the economy to flourish.

These amenities can be made available only by sacrificing some of the greenery. If the building of large dams is to be halted in response to the environmentalists' agitations, where are the additional foodgrains, irrigation facilities and uninterrupted power for industry to come from?

■ ■ ■

Learning from our Failures as well as Success

There is no finality about failure, said Jawaharlal Nehru. Perhaps, that is why learning from failure is easier than learning from success, as success often appears to be the last step of the ladder. Possibilities of life, however, are endless and there are worlds beyond the stars—which is literally true. What appears as success in one moment may turn out to be a failure or even worse in the next moment.

We often do not know what is failure and what is success ultimately.

There are examples of people who became wealthy but renounced all their wealth achieved after a lifetime's effort. The kings like Bharthrihari gave up their kingdoms because of their failure in love. The Duke of Windsor abdicated the throne of England for marrying an American divorcee Miss Simpson.

While we can see our failures clearly, success is prone to blind our vision. Yet, the time-world where we live in is a mixture of pain and pleasure, sorrow and delight, light and darkness, success and failure! Success as well as failure are parts of our life and experience. We gain from both and also lose from both. Failure dejects us, success delights us, but experience accretes them both. After a while, success also loses its shine just as failure loses its sting. An aware person learns from both successes and failures of life and begins to see life what it is?

Most people try to achieve what they want. They either

fail or succeed in getting what they want. In a difficult world trial and error become our way of solving life's problems. Yet, there are escapists who avoid undertaking the trial because they are scared of meeting failure or committing the error. They, perhaps, consider making mistake as wrong and harmful but the fact is that, for most of us, trial and error are both helpful and necessary.

Error provides the feedback for building the ladder to success. Error pushes one to put together a new and better trial, leading through more errors and trials, hopefully, finding ultimately a workable and creative solution. To meet an error is only a temporary, and often necessary part of the process that leads to success or well-earned achievement. No errors or failures, often, means no success either. This is more true in business and while handling an on-going project.

According to some business training programmes, an early partial success is not commended. In fact, early success in a long-term project is regarded as a premature outcome of good efforts that is likely to cause complaisant and slackening of effort to achieve the ultimate objective of the project. Early success might tempt one to get fixed on to what seem to have worked so quickly and easily and stop looking up any further. Later, maybe, a competitor will learn from the slackened 'achiever' to further explore for larger possibilities and push on to find a much better solution that will push the earlier achiever out of the competition.

Yet, there are many organizations who believe in what they call 'culture of perfection: a set of organizational beliefs that any failure is unacceptable'. Only a hundred per cent, untainted success will be acceptable. "To retain your reputation as an achiever, you must reach every goal and never, ever make a mistake that you can't hide or blame on someone else."

But this is a flawed strategy because the stress and terror in such an organization, at some point, become unbearable and lead to attrition. The ceaseless covering up of small blemishes, finger-pointing and shifting the blame result into rapid turnover, as people rise high, then fall abruptly from grace. Meanwhile, lying, cheating, falsifying of data, and hiding of problems go on and swings and shake the organization from crisis to crisis and, ultimately, weaken it irreparably.

Some ego-driven, 'experienced' achievers forget that time and environment have changed and demand other kinds of inputs. A senior lecturer of ten years' standing was rejected and one with only one-year experience was selected. When the senior protested, selectors told him: "You too have only one year of experience—only repeated ten times. The selected lecturer has fresher and more relevant experience."

Balance counts and a little failure may help to preserve one's perspective on success. Finally, life is more than a count of failures and successes, as a humorist said "try and try—only twice, the third time let some one else try" is yet another way of looking at life's struggle.

■ ■ ■

Global Warming

Global warming is when the earth heats up (the temperature rises). It happens when greenhouse gases (carbon dioxide, water vapor, nitrous oxide, and methane) trap heat and light from the sun in the earth's atmosphere, which increases the temperature. This hurts many people, animals, and plants. Many cannot take the change, so they die.

What is the Greenhouse Effect?

The greenhouse effect is when the temperature rises because the sun's heat and light is trapped in the earth's atmosphere. This is like when heat is trapped in a car. On a very hot day, the car gets hotter when it is out in the parking lot. This is because the heat and light from the sun can get into the car, by going through the windows, but it can't get back out. This is what the greenhouse effect does to the earth. The heat and light can get through the atmosphere, but it can't get out. As a result, the temperature rises.

The sun's heat can get into the car through the windows but is then trapped. This makes what ever the place might be, a greenhouse, a car, a building, or the earth's atmosphere, hotter. This diagram shows the heat coming into a car as visible light (light you can see) and infrared light (heat). Once the light is inside the car, it is trapped and the heat builds up, just like it does in the earth's atmosphere.

What are Greenhouse Gasses?

Greenhouse gasses are gasses are in the earth's atmosphere

that collect heat and light from the sun. With too many greenhouse gasses in the air, the earth's atmosphere will trap too much heat and the earth will get too hot. As a result people, animals, and plants would die because the heat would be too strong.

What is Global Warming doing to the Environment?

Global warming is affecting many parts of the world. Global warming makes the sea rise, and when the sea rises, the water covers many low land islands. This is a big problem for many of the plants, animals, and people on islands. The water covers the plants and causes some of them to die. When they die, the animals lose a source of food, along with their habitat. Although animals have a better ability to adapt to what happens than plants do, they may die also. When the plants and animals die, people lose two sources of food, plant food and animal food. They may also lose their homes. As a result, they would also have to leave the area or die. This would be called a break in the food chain, or a chain reaction, one thing happening that leads to another and so on.

The oceans are affected by global warming in other ways, as well. Many things that are happening to the ocean are linked to global warming. One thing that is happening is warm water, caused from global warming, is harming and killing algae in the ocean.

Global warming is doing many things to people as well as animals and plants. It is killing algae, but it is also destroying many huge forests. The pollution that causes global warming is linked to acid rain. Acid rain gradually destroys almost everything it touches. Global warming is also causing many more fires that wipe out whole forests.

This happens because global warming can make the earth very hot. In forests, some plants and trees leaves can be so dry that they catch on fire.

What Causes Global Warming?

Many things cause global warming. One thing that causes global warming is electrical pollution. Electricity causes pollution in many ways, some worse than others. In most cases, fossil fuels are burned to create electricity. Fossil fuels are made of dead plants and animals. Some examples of fossil fuels are oil and petroleum. Many pollutants (chemicals that pollute the air, water, and land) are sent into the air when fossil fuels are burned. Some of these chemicals are called greenhouse gasses.

We use these sources of energy much more than the sources that give off less pollution. Petroleum, one of the sources of energy, is used a lot. It is used for transportation, making electricity, and making many other things. Although this source of energy gives off a lot of pollution, it is used for 38% of the United States' energy.

Some other examples of using energy and polluting the air are:

- Turning on a light
- Watching T.V.
- Listening to a stereo
- Washing or drying clothes
- Using a hair dryer
- Riding in a car
- Heating a meal in the microwave
- Using an air conditioner

Global Warming 153

- Playing a video game
- Using a dish washer

When you do these things, you are causing more greenhouse gasses to be sent into the air. Greenhouse gasses are sent into the air because creating the electricity you use to do these things causes pollution. If you think of how many times a day you do these things, it's a lot. You even have to add in how many other people do these things! That turns out to be a lot of pollutants going into the air a day because of people like us using electricity. The least amount of electricity you use, the better.

When we throw our garbage away, the garbage goes to landfills. Landfills are those big hills that you go by on an expressway that stink. They are full of garbage. The garbage is then sometimes burned. This sends an enormous amount of greenhouse gasses into the air and makes global warming worse.

Another thing that makes global warming worse is when people cut down trees. Trees and other plants collect carbon dioxide (CO2), which is a greenhouse gas.

What are Some of the other Dangerous Chemicals?

Some other chemicals that cause air pollution and are bad for the environment and people are:

Ozone: Ozone is produced when other pollution chemicals combine. It is the basic element of smog. It causes many different kinds of health issues dealing with the lungs. It can damage plants and limit sight. It can also cause a lot of property damage.

VOC's (volatile organic compounds, smog formers): VOC's are let into the air when fuel is burned. This chemical can cause cancer. It can also harm plants.

NOx (nitrogen dioxide): This chemical forms smog. It is also formed by burning sources of energy, like gas, coal, and oil, and by cars. This chemical causes problems in the respiratory system (including the lungs). It causes acid rain, and it can damage trees. This chemical can eat away buildings and statues.

CO (carbon monoxide): The source of this chemical is burning sources of energy. It causes blood vessel problems and respiratory failures.

PM-10 (particulate matter): The source of this chemical is plowing and burning down fields. It can cause death and lung damage. It can make it hard for people to breathe. The smoke, soot, ash, and dust formed by this chemical can make many cities dirty.

Sulfur Dioxide: This chemical is produced by making paper and metals. This chemical can cause permanent lung damage. It can cause acid rain which kills trees and damages building and statues.

Lead: This chemical is in paint, leaded gasoline, smelters, and in lead storage batteries. It can cause many brain and nerve damages and digestive problems.

■■■

India's Urban Scenario

Contrary to popular concepts of a predominantly rural India, an increasingly larger percentage of Indian population today lives in the urban areas. India's urban population is now second largest in the world after China, and is higher than the total urban population of all countries put together barring China, USA and Russia. Over the last fifty years, while the country's population has grown by 2.5 times, in the urban areas it has grown by five times.

In 1947, only 60 million people (15 per cent of the total population at that time) lived in urban areas. India's urban population grew from the 290 million reported in the 2001 Census to an estimated 340 million in 2008 (30 per cent of the total population) and it could soar to 590 million plus (40 per cent of the population) by 2030.

This urban expansion will happen at a speed quite unlike anything India has seen before. The steep growth in number of people living is partly due to the skewed development that has led to proliferation of commercial activities, and greater job opportunities in towns and cities.

Facilities like health and education, and infrastructure like roadways, telecommunication, airports, railways and ports are also many times better in urban areas.

In spite of its prominent role in Indian Economy, urban India faces serious problems due to population pressure, deterioration in the physical environment and quality of life. According to estimates, nearly one third of the urban India lives below poverty line. About 15 per cent of the urbanites do not have access to safe drinking water and about 50 per cent are not covered by sanitary facilities.

Traffic congestion has assumed critical dimensions in many metropolitan cities due to massive increase in the number of personal vehicles, inadequate road space and lack of public transport.

There is a huge and widening gap between demand and supply of essential services and infrastructure. Urban poor in India are forced to live under unhygienic conditions in slums, lacking in basic amenities. Slums have grown in almost all major cities due to inability of major chunks of population to afford accommodation in planned areas of the cities.

The five fold explosive growth in urban India has resulted in serious infrastructure constraints. Water, transport, housing, electricity, health and sanitation are some of the areas of concern. Infrastructure to meet these requirements calls for huge investments.

Cities offer the promise of a higher quality of life for a large number of Indians. They are also vital for funding the development because they generate 80-85 per cent of tax revenue. Urban India is today failing many of its citizens.

Across all major quality-of-life indicators, cities of India fall much short of delivering even a basic standard of living to the residents. As per the MGI report, if India continues to invest in urban infrastructure at its current rate—very low by international standards—in 20 years' time the urban infrastructure will fall woefully short of what is necessary to sustain prosperous cities.

Life of the city dweller would become a lot tougher.

Water shortage will result in a large section of the population having no access to potable water. More than 70 per cent of the sewage will remain untreated, causing serious health problems. Increasing number of private vehicles and shortcomings in the public transportation infrastructure would create urban gridlock—similar to the acute congestion that cripples some Latin American cities.

Funding

The MGI (McKinsey Global Institute) report suggests four sources of funding that India should tap into—monetizing land assets, collecting higher property taxes and user charges that reflect costs, debt and public-private partnerships, and formula-based government funding.

Governance

India's large cities are still governed by bureaucrats who can be transferred out of office at a short notice. This is in sharp contrast to large cities world-wide where the mayors have been empowered with long tenures and clear accountability.

According to the MGI report, fully formed metropolitan authorities with clearly defined roles are absolutely essential for the successful management of large cities.

Planning

India's urban planning is in very poor state. There are urban plans but they are not practical, are rarely followed and are riddled with exemptions.

As per the MGI report, central to planning in any city is the optimal allocation of space, especially land use and Floor Area Ratio (FAR) planning. These plans need to be detailed, comprehensive and enforceable, and exemptions should be rare.

Sectoral Policies

All good cities have policies in critical areas like job creation, affordable housing for low-income groups, public transportation and climate-change mitigation. As per the MGI report, India has largely failed to embrace the need for dedicated policy attention within cities. In the absence of policy to meet the housing needs of low-income group, Indian cities will continue to be effected by the slum menace.

Shape

India has to aim for a distributed model of urbanization to ensure its federal structure as also to ensure that migration flows are not unbalanced towards a particular city or cities. MGI report concludes that India should build at least 25 new satellite cities near today's Tier 1 and 2 cities to accommodate populations in each of up to one million people.

Such an effort, despite being more expensive than renewing existing cities, will act as a benchmark and a model for well-planned, environmentally sustainable world-class cities, while helping ease of the strains of rapid urbanization.

Constitution (Seventy-Fourth Amendment) Act 1992

This is a revolutionary piece of legislation by which Constitution of India was amended to incorporate a separate Chapter on urban local bodies, which seeks to redefine their role, power, function and finances. The salient features of this Act are:

Urban local bodies, to be known as Municipal Corporations, Municipal Councils and Nagar Panchayat depending on the population shall be constituted through universal adult franchise in each notified urban area of the country.

These shall be constituted for a period of five years and if dissolved earlier, an election to reconstitute it shall be completed before the expiration of a period of six months from the date of its dissolution. Not less than one-third of total number of seats in each urban local body shall be reserved for women.

The Legislature of a State may by law entrust on these bodies such power and authority as may be necessary to enable them to function as institution of local self government, including those listed in the Twelfth Schedule.

The Twelfth Schedule of the Constitution has listed the following functions of the urban local bodies:

- Urban Planning including town planning.
- Regulation of land-use and construction of buildings.
- Planning for economic and social development.
- Roads and bridges.
- Water supply for domestic, industrial and commercial purposes.
- Public health, sanitation, conservancy and solid waste management.
- Fire services.
- Urban forestry, protection of the environment and promotion of ecological aspects.
- Safeguarding the interests of weaker sections of society, including the handicapped and mentally retarded.

- Slum improvement and up-gradation.
- Urban poverty alleviation.
- Provision of Urban amenities and facilities such as parks, gardens, playgrounds.
- Promotion of cultural, educational and aesthetic aspects.
- Burials and burial grounds; cremations, cremation grounds and electric crematoriums.
- Cattle pounds; prevention of cruelty to animals.
- Vital statistics including registration of births and deaths.
- Public amenities including street lighting, parking lots, bus stops and public conveniences.
- Regulation of slaughter houses and tanneries.

■ ■ ■

How Safe are Mobile Phones?

Millions of people own a mobile phone these days, and ever since they have been around scientists question the fact of they are safe or not. Do they cause tumors, earaches, mercury poisoning? All these health risks are mentioned in every article I found.

But nowhere could I find anything that was sure if mobiles did cause all of the above. This is where science fails us. The problem is that mobile phones are still too new to know the long-term effects on human.

Mobile phones give of a radiation of radio frequency round 10 MHz to 300 Ghz. But so do other appliances. Why does mobiles especially get put in the picture of being hazardous? Soon it will be clear whether the radio frequency emissions from mobiles cause health effect.

Drivers who use there mobiles whilst driving are the only "health risk" that can be proven, the drivers get distracted and lose control over the vehicle. Technology invented something for this, hands-free sets.

But now the question is do those hands free sets really solve the problem? Researchers now are looking at if the hands free sets don't cause other problems.

A report from the magazine "which?" said that hands free kits raised levels if radiation to the head from mobile phones by up to three and a half times. The consumer association immediately stressed that it had done no research into this whether this radiation could cause damage to the brain.

That just proves that whenever there has been research a report is released to prove that research wrong. Probably is done not to cause any chaos.

Mobiles are said to cause brain tumors, they say this because there was found to be more tumors of the same kind amongst mobile phone users. Mobiles cause memory loss, radiation sickness.

Mobiles can disturb your sleep pattern, according to the researchers from the university of Zurich, mobile phones increases brain activity during our sleep. A really strange result of the use of mobile phones is that mobile phones can release the poisonous mercury from fillings causing brain damage, scientist say this is due to the electrical fields given off by mobile phones can activate the mercury, giving off a gas.

The fumes attach the nervous system causing conditions from depression, asthma to Alzheimer's disease and multiple sclerosis.

Some studies have suggested links between Radio frequency radiation and lymphoma, microwaves and memory loss, mobile phone use and a rare type of brain cancer, mobile phone radiation and DNA destruction, and mobile phone use and damaged scalp nerves.

The World Health Organization has asked for more and more research, but all the time and money spent results in the same answer over and over again.

When the press publishes such reports, that these studies came up without result the scientists will report that their data suggest it is unlikely mobile phones cause cancer, perhaps even highly unlikely. They will admit that they cannot rule out and effect.

How Safe are Mobile Phones?

This may satisfy the public, until a counter report is published. How ever if these studies can identify a mechanism that causes the brain tumors, we have a real public health threat on our hands and the authorities are put into action.

End of fear is when we stop using our mobiles or we stop using them in a way that could be dangerous.

It seems one can't enjoy technology any more without its faithful side effects, suffering a slow death. All these risks are know to effect the youth more.

If that is known why do mobile phone company's make their phones with Disney covers and with other accessories to make mobiles more popular to the youth.

Even scarier is the thought that those companies may not be telling us the whole truth. If mobile phones are questioned now, when will it be stopped? Will microwaves, electric blankets, or televisions be next?

Technology is doing every thing it can to improve the mobile phones. To try and make the radiation that is sent out as harmless as possible, in the mean time before the technological level is high enough to do so, experts have made reports to reduce the amount of radiation. They recommend things like:

- Cut down on time spent using the mobile phone
- Use a mobile phone where the antenna is mounted outside a car
- Keep mobile at a short distance from the ear

Factors that can effect how people perceive how risky new technology is that no one really knows what the long-term effects are, and until that is certain people will still be researching new possibilities. If no immediate link is put between all the risks and the real effect of mobile phones on humans, then there will be no problem in buying mobiles.

The problem is that without knowing the really risk manufactures cannot develop mobiles to being safer, so many people are exposed to harmful radiation without that individual knowing. As we know from the past only big helpful research starts when a tragedy hits. In other words, who knows?

There is no proof that mobile phones are a health risk, or that they are a hundred percent safe. Some say the danger does not end until after ten minutes after hanging up because the user is still processing the conversation.

■■■

Should Steroids Be Banned?

It is amazing what athletes will do to achieve higher levels of performance and to sometimes get the extra edge on the competition. Most of the time people do not realize the long-term effects that result from the decisions they make early in life. This resembles the use of steroids in a person's life.

Steroids became an option to athletes in the Olympics and other major sporting events during the 1950's. But this use of steroids among athletes only became widely apparent when Canadian sprint runner Ben Johnson tested positive for steroid use after winning the gold medal for the one hundred-meter dash during the 1988 Olympics.

Now a skinny fifteen-year-old can just walk down to the local gym and find people who either sell or know how to get in contact with those who sell the drug that will make him envious of his friends.

Steroids are an attractive drug. While steroids seem harmless to the unaware user, they can have a risky effect.

Most of the time whether the users are new or experienced, they do not know the dangerous consequences steroids can have on their bodies and their minds.

Though steroids cause a relatively insignificant number of deaths in our society, the banning of steroids is justified because steroids have a lot of side effects not known to the uninformed user.

Even though steroids are known as a somewhat dangerous substance, they are legal to have and to consume. There has not been a study that proves such possible side effects are linked to medical problems of steroid users.

There are those who have pointed out several cases where someone has died and an autopsy has shown that the person was using steroids, but they claim this does not mean that it is a deadly drug as some medical professionals have stated.

Some advocates of steroids believe that because steroids are legal, and because it is the decision of the user to take the drug, steroids are not causing a problem in society.

Alcohol and cigarettes are consumed by millions of people, causing a lot of deteriorating effects on their bodies, but there has never been a ban on these items because of the dangers that they can cause. Why should steroids be different?

Some people say that the wide spread use of steroids among athletes is forcing the young athletes to use steroids, even though it is against their standards.

This is because they know they can not compete at the level against their opponents who are using steroids to go to the next level of performance. A lot of people claim that this is how competition is supposed to be. Race car drivers are out there every day, pushing themselves to the limit.

They are taking that corner a little bit faster, putting themselves in danger just a little bit more. This is no different than the risk football players, wrestlers, and weight lifters take when they decide to use steroids to take them to the next level. There are the people who justify steroid abuse because of these reasons, claiming that their use in sports and other activities are just the added element that an athlete needs to boost their performance.

However, there has not yet been any definite medical research to prove that steroid abuse is linked to severe medical conditions.

Only the warnings that come from users that are currently dealing with medical difficulties that most likely have been a result of steroid use. These people are living proof of the harmful effects of steroids.

Cigarettes and alcohol are major contributors to thousands of deaths each year. A lot of people have family members or friends that are suffering from diseases and health conditions cause by smoking and drinking.

Sometimes these can lead to an early grave, sometimes a very painful death. Some people will use these situations as a reason not to drink or smoke.

A similar situation would be a young athlete watching their muscular idols suffering from medical problems caused by steroids.

Some of these professionals will even admit to their former steroid abuse in hopes to persuade the thousands of young athletes that the quick results of steroids do not pay off in the end. When these kids see the long-term results that occur to professional athletes, they should realize the need to stay away from steroids or give up the addiction that they have to them.

This might mean they will have to give up the idea of the body that they have always dreamed of. If someone who was currently abusing steroids was to listen to what a former addict has gone through, that person might very well be persuaded to give up the addiction.

In the end these people would have the advantage because they will be the ones who are going to live a longer and happier life.

Steroids are also becoming more common in women's athletics. The doses of steroids that women will take when they are cycling on steroids can have a lot of dangerous side effects.

Some of the short-term effects involve deepened voice, loss of scalp hair, growth of facial hair and chest hair, and also genital problems. Women may also have irregularities in their menstrual cycle. The long-term side effects for women have not been determined yet.

Even with all of these effects, steroid use is very common in the sports world. Athletes who use steroids do not think of themselves as cheaters. Many set high goals for themselves and work hard at achieving them.

Steroids are seen as just a way to help them work harder and more effectively. Athletes that do not use steroids know that steroid users have an unfair advantage.

United States shot-putter Augie Wolf summarized many athletes' feelings: "Drug taking is rampant. Only the uninformed get caught. The pressure to take drugs is enormous.

If professional athletes are taking steroids, then a high school athlete has to be kicking the thought around of trying steroids. They have to wonder how they are going to succeed if they do not take them. Steroid use could possibly be lowered in high school age kids if their high school physical education teachers taught their students about the effects of steroids and the lifestyle it could lead to.

Just because there is no official proof that steroids can damage and possibly kill is no reason to allow steroids to be legal in out society. No proof does not mean that the dangers do not exist. Every year more and more famous retired athletes are admitting to steroid use in their career, and admitting certain medical problems as a result of their steroid abuse. People need to listen to what they have to say, and use them as the example for teaching the younger crowd. The banning of steroids would not only help the people who are currently abusing them, but also it help taper the spread of addiction to steroids in society.

■ ■ ■

Corruption and Quality of Governance

That India is one of the most corrupt countries in the world is not the news, the news is that there is no hope for any respite from this evil which is essentially an anti-poor phenomenon. According to the Transparency International, India ranks very high on the Corruption Perception Index. There are a lot of things because of which one is proud of being an Indian. However, there are a lot more for which one is ashamed of being an Indian, and corruption is one of them.

Courage, integrity and moral values of life have been major casualties in recent times. We have seen how these qualities have nose-dived to absurdly low depths. Our leaders have lost total sense of responsibilities and propriety and have misused and abused the power and authority vested in them with impunity, and with utter disregard to public interests.

They have literally converted the governmental infrastructure as their personal fiefdom, resulting in series of scams and scandals. As a natural aftermath of this degradation on moral values and quality of leadership, everyday life of common citizens has become a living hell. Municipal services are heaped in corruption and inefficiency, with erratic electricity and water supply, choked and overflowing sewers, smelly drains, neglected roads and streets with potholes, and dotted with rotting garbage dumps and stinking public toilets.

Standards of education in government schools and colleges have gone down and several money spinning private schools and coaching centres have mushroomed, whose sole aim is to fleece the public.

In the present economic scenario, the basic prerequisites of an efficient administrative system, conducive and growth-oriented environment and good and reliable infrastructure are not available in our governing apparatus, which are essential for a sound economy. Inefficient and inapt administration, which has no work-culture worth the name, and which is forever on holiday or holiday-mood, has caused serious overruns on development projects, resulting in losses and chronic shortages of power, roads, ports and means of communication.

Family-planning programmes have failed miserably, which has led to further inadequacies of our basic facilities—education, health, housing and transport projects. Perennial shortage in our infrastructure network has stunted our industrial and commercial growth. Absence of right environments has failed the system and driven out our intellectuals to greener pastures in foreign lands, thereby causing brain-drain.

Even our space programmes have been jeopardized due to flight of scientific talent. Our industrialists have also failed the nation. Inspite of prolonged protection from foreign competition, they have not developed the indigenous technology and have remained heavily dependent on outdated imported technologies to produce substandard products, most of which cannot compete in international markets either in price or in quality.

The root cause of all this is our poor work-culture and corrupt practices, which have now become endemic in our national character. The main aim of the bulk of our citizens is to make hay while the sun shines and not to worry about the nation and its plebeian designs.

Our political system has proved to be the fountainhead of corruption. During elections, help of industrial and business houses and criminal elements are invited to fund the extravagant election expenses of candidates and use muscle power to muster votes, which results in nexus between politicians, business houses and underground mafia. This nexus associates are later reimbursed through scams and scandals by siphoning off public funds.

Huge amounts received from international agencies for welfare projects are pilfered and shared among the nexus associates of the politicians in power. The bureaucracy has been made servile through carrot and stick policy.

In fact, most of them have now become conduit for slush money for their political bosses, and in process have become drain into the vortex and are partners in promoting corruption. They have forgotten the legacy of courage, integrity and uprightness of their predecessors—the Indian Civil Services cadre of yore. They have forgotten that their first duty is to serve the people and not their self-interests or their political bosses.

Corruption is an anti-poor phenomenon which can only be tackled by better governance and less government. Apart from its moral and ethical dimension, corruption is the major cause of poor becoming poorer and, of course, rich getting converted into super rich or filthy and vulgar rich.

In democratic setup, and in a plural economy like ours, everyone is guaranteed the right to grow to one's potential and create wealth by all legitimate means. However, corruption of any kind deprives the common man from 'climbing' the next ladder and he either continues at the same or slides further down to a more pathetic condition.

Corruption is really anti-poor. 31.5% of the food grains and 36% of sugar in the Public Distribution System (PDS) gets diverted to black market. The fact is that Rs. 20,000 crore is the subsidy involved in the PDS and 30% leaks to the black market, in other words, more than Rs. 6,000 crore are made available for the politicians, corrupt officials of the PDS, the corrupt shopkeepers and their protectors. We can, therefore, see how, while in the name of the poor, an argument can be made for food security and subsidy.

Different scams have shown the linkage between antinational elements. 300 people died in Mumbai blast in 1993 and this was made possible because RDX could be smuggled by bribing Rs 20 lakh to certain Custom officials. We can, therefore, see that corruption is anti-economic development, anti-poor and anti-national.

What is corruption and why should any government and its people fight corruption? The World Bank definition of corruption is "Use of public office for private profit". Some or all government offices are public, and the use of these offices for 'private profit' by politicians, bureaucrats and the others is common in India. So much so, we have created such systems in our country that corruption has become endemic. Like Mark Twain's statement that every one talks about the weather but nobody seems to be able to do anything about it, **the entire nation talks about corruption but nobody is able to do anything about it.**

Former Central Vigilance Commissioner, N. Vittal, used to compare corruption with a disease like AIDS. He felt as AIDS is the result of uncontrolled sexual behaviour, corruption is the outcome of uncontrolled financial behaviour.

The next aspect to be understood is why the government and responsible citizens must fight corruption? The straight forward answer is, because corruption is anti-poor and anti-development.

The Human Development Report for South-Asia, pointed out that if India's level of corruption could be brought down to the Scandinavian countries, its GDP will improve by 1.5% and foreign bank investment by 12%.

Anything that is anti-poor and hence anti-social must be on top of the government agenda to rectify the situation, but in a country where populism takes priority over good governance, it doesn't find even a mention.

It is often said that leaders of India have deliberately kept the people ignorant so that they won't know how badly they are governed. The present state of anarchy has made everyday life of the citizens a living hell. They not only live in the fear of life and property, they also have to make do with inefficiency in every government department.

Perhaps, the present state of affairs can be described in the words of Mahatma Gandhi whose understanding of India and patriotism cannot be challenged. "India is a country of self-suppression and timidity", he said.

This contributes to a common man's low expectations from anything Indian, including the administration. Many intellectuals who are painted by others 'as full of self-loathing', perhaps also contribute to this phenomenon—that nothing can be done to eradicate corruption and we have to resign to our destiny and fate. It is not true. Of course, a lot can be done, provided there is a will to change the present state of affairs.

Mahatma Gandhi's dream was to see India with every face without a tear. Alas, in more than 60 years, we have not been able to meet the aspirations and objective potential of our people. Official figures indicate that at least 36% live

below the austerely defined by the Planning Commission. Today, millions of our citizens do not have the elementary freedom from economic poverty, social deprivation or political tyranny. As famous Nobel Laureate Amartya Sen will like us to understand, we are only technically free but not truly free.

■ ■ ■

Education for All

The gains achieved since the Education for All and Millennium Development Goals were adopted in 2000 are undeniable: great strides have been made towards universal primary education, increased participation in secondary and tertiary education and, in many countries, gender equality. More widely, there have been improvements in overcoming hunger, poverty, and child and maternal mortality.

The global financial crisis could radically change all this. Reaching the marginalized demonstrates that declining government revenue and rising unemployment now pose a serious threat to progress in all areas of human development. Government budgets are under even greater pressure and funding for education is especially vulnerable. So are poor households. Rising poverty levels mean that the challenge of meeting basic human needs is a daily struggle. Lessons from the past teach us that children are often the first to suffer—as is their chance to go to school.

Global Monitoring Report, 2010, underscores that there is a long way to travel. There are still at least 72 million children worldwide who are missing out on their right to education because of the simple fact of where they are born or who their family is. Millions of youths leave school without the skills they need to succeed in the workforce and one in six adults is denied the right to literacy.

The 2010 Report is a call to action. We must reach the marginalized. Only inclusive education systems have the potential to harness the skills needed to build the knowledge societies of the twenty-first century.

The international community needs to identify the threat to education posed by the economic crisis and the rise in global food prices. Human development indicators are deteriorating. An estimated 125 million additional people could be pushed into malnutrition and 90 million into poverty in 2010.

With poverty rising, unemployment growing and remittances diminishing, many poor and vulnerable households are being forced to cut back on education spending or withdraw their children from school. National budgets in poor countries are under pressure. Sub-Saharan Africa faces a potential loss of around US$4.6 billion annually in financing for education in 2009 and 2010, equivalent to a 10% reduction in spending per primary-school pupil.

As part of an effective response, it is need of the hour to provide sustained and predictable aid to counteract revenue losses, protect priority social spending and support progress in education.

The situation is not hopeless everywhere, though. Some countries have achieved extraordinary advances. Benin started out in 1999 with one of the world's lowest net enrollment ratios but may now be on track for universal primary education by 2015. The share of girls out of school has declined from 58% to 54%, and the gender gap in primary education is narrowing in many countries. Between 1985–1994 and 2000–2007, the adult literacy rate increased by 10%, to its current level of 84%. The number of adult female literates has increased at a faster pace than that of males.

However, much need to be done. Malnutrition affects around 175 million young children each year and is a health and an education emergency. There were 72 million children out of school in 2007. Business as usual would leave 56 million children out of school in 2015.

Around 54% of children out of school are girls. In sub-Saharan Africa, almost 12 million girls may never enrol. In Yemen, nearly 80% of girls out of school are unlikely ever to enrol, compared with 36% of boys. Literacy remains among the most neglected of all education goals, with about 759 million adults lacking literacy skills today. Two-thirds are women.

Millions of children are leaving school without having acquired basic skills. In some countries in sub-Saharan Africa, young adults with five years of education had a 40% probability of being illiterate. In the Dominican Republic, Ecuador and Guatemala, fewer than half of grade 3 students had more than very basic reading skills. Some 1.9 million new teacher posts will be required to meet universal primary education by 2015.

Education Scenario of India

Literacy in India has made remarkable strides since Independence. This has been further confirmed by the results of the Census 2001. The literacy rate has increased from 18.33% in 1951 to 64.84% in 2001. This is despite the fact that during the major part of the last five decades there has been exponential growth of the population at nearly 2% per annum.

The Indian Constitution resolves to provide quality education to all and, in an effort to fulfill the educational needs of the country, specifically for the diverse societies and cultures of the country, the government has chalked out different educational categories: elementary education, secondary education, higher education, adult education, technical and vocational education. Free and compulsory education to all children up to the age of fourteen years is now a constitutional commitment in India. Despite serious handicaps of means and resources, the country has built up during the last 50 years a very large system of education, and has created a vast body of men and women equipped with a high order of scientific and technological capabilities, robust humanist and philosophical thought and creativity.

The Government of India has initiated a number of programmes to achieve the goal of Universalization of Elementary Education (UEE), from among which the *Sarva Shiksha Abhiyan* (SSA), launched in 2001, is the most recent one. It aimed at achieving universal elementary education of satisfactory quality by 2010. The SSA is expected to generate demand for secondary education in view of which the Government of India has recently launched the *Rashtriya Madhyamik Shiksha Abhiyan* (RMSA) to improve universal access and quality at the Secondary and Higher Secondary stages of education.

The elementary education system of India has expanded into one of the largest in the world. Number of primary schools increased from 2.15 lakhs in 1950-51 to 6.1 lakhs in 1997-98; the corresponding increase in upper primary schools was from 0.14 lakhs to 1.85 lakhs. These 8.17 lakh schools together enrolled 1,110 lakh children as compared to 192 lakh in 1951.

Universal provision of education has been substantially

achieved at the primary stage (classes I-V). An estimated 95 percent of the rural population living in 8,26,000 habitations has a primary school within a walking distance of one km and about 85 per cent of the rural population has an upper primary school within a walking distance of three km. More than 150 million children are currently enrolled covering around 90 per cent of the children in the age group of 6-14 years. Recent surveys on literacy rates indicate a phenomenal progress in the nineties and indicate a significant rise in the literacy level.

Despite such significant achievements in the recent years, it is realized that there are serious problems of gender, regional, sectional and caste disparities in UEE. A significant proportion of children continue to drop out due to socioeconomic and cultural factors as also due to lack of adequate infrastructure, shortage of teachers and unsatisfactory quality of education provided.

Linked to the overall issue of education is the sub-issue of value education. It is feared that the more we industrialize, greater will be the need for value education at all levels. Although, we have been led to believe that India's values are the best, the western values are associated with progress, development, quick achievement, and hence are being readily imbibed by the students. It has to be understood that there is no particular set of values which guarantees success and that the societal values must match with the organizational values and hence, values such as wisdom, humility, rationality, intellectualism etc. will have to be inculcated in education at all levels. In this context, India's cultural values will need to be integrated with education.

■ ■ ■

Widespread Influence of Mahatma Gandhi

There is not a single country in the whole world where the name of Mahatma Gandhi is not known. He became famous because he dedicated his whole life to the service of the motherland, and service of humanity. Gandhi's father Karamchand Gandhi, popularly known as Kaba, was a Minister there in Porbandar, in Gujarat. His wife Putalibai was a extremely religious women. She would not have her meal until she had worshipped the sun. To these parents a son was born on October 2nd, 1869. He was their youngest son. He was called Mohandas.

As his father was in Rajkot at that time, he attended the school there. Being extremely shy, he did not mix with the other children. Most of the time he kept to himself. At that time he was 18 years old.

Everyone in the family decided that he should go to England and become a Barrister, so that on his return he could become a Dewan like his father. Respecting their wishes, Gandhi set sail for England in 1888.

However, he soon got adjusted to the new environment. He returned to India in 1891, after the completion of his studies. After qualifying as a Barrister, he set up his practice as a lawyer, in Rajkot. As he did not get much work there, he came to Bombay (Now Mumbai). Even in Bombay he did not get any cases. Finally, he got one case. He prepared well for it, but in court he was unable to present it satisfactorily. Disappointed, he felt he would never make a successful lawyer. Just at that time Gandhi's elder brother managed to get him a case. He was asked to represent Mr. Abdulla, a rich businessman in South Africa. After much deliberation, Gandhi agreed to accept the case. He left his homeland and set sail for Africa in 1895. Although there were many Indians staying in Africa at that time, all the power was in the hands of the British people. They considered themselves superior, and treated the Indians and the natives in a most insulting manner. Gandhi undertook Abdulla's case and handled it very well.

The Indians were very much impressed, and wanted Gandhi to stay on in Africa. However, he was treated very badly by the British people. Wherever he went, he had to face insults and rudeness. At times, he was even physically assaulted. One day, when he was traveling from Durban to Pretoria in the first class compartment of a train, a British man boarded the compartment. On seeing Gandhi, the British man got furious. He called the Railway officer, and both ordered him to get out of the train.

Since Gandhi had purchased a first class ticket, he refused to do so. Finally the police were summoned. They pushed him out of the compartment and threw his luggage out of the window. Gandhi had to spend the whole night on the platform. He had decided to return to India on the completion of his work in Africa, but the plight of the Indians there disturbed him greatly. He resolved to stay, and fight the unjust and inhuman laws that were imposed on them. For everywhere there was discrimination. There was one set of rules for the Indians and natives, and a different set for the British people.

Gandhi gave considerable thought to the matter. He realized that to fight against injustice it was vital for the

Widespread Influence of Mahatma Gandhi

people to have unity amongst themselves. He tried very hard to bring about this unity. He organized many meetings, and made the people aware of the situation. In reply, the people appointed him as their leader, and agreed to be guided by him.

Since all the power was in the hands of the English people, Gandhi realized that to fight them it was necessary to use an entirely different method. It was then that he thought of the novel idea of 'Satyagraha'. Satyagraha insistence on truth, a non violent protest against injustice. His movement aimed at fighting the many unjust laws that were imposed on them, and for it to be successful, he was prepared to face all hardships and obstacles. It was no easy task. He suffered much humiliation, faced many problems, but he did not give up. It was during this time that a war broke out between the British and the Dutch settlers in Africa. It was known as the Boer War.

Gandhi and other Indians gave whatever help they could to the British. The British won the war, and taking into consideration the help Gandhi had rendered to them, they gave the Indians more privileges. They also agreed to abolish the unjust laws that were imposed on them. Gandhi felt very happy that his stay in Africa.

By the time all these developments took place in Africa, it was 1914. Gandhi had spent almost 20 years in that country. He returned to India, for he had made up his mind to fight for the freedom of India. He decided that he would not miss a single opportunity that would help him in serving his country and countrymen.

As such he toured the whole of India, and brought an awakening in the people living in villages and towns. North of the Ganges, near the boundary of Nepal, was a small place called Champaranya. It was noted for its cultivation of Indigo dye. Unfortunately, the British planters in Champaranya treated the local workers most cruelly. Worse still, the Government paid little heed to the workers cries. With the result that they were utterly disgusted with their employers, Gandhi heard of this and went to Champaranya to do something for them. He was unable to bear their miserable plight. He began a satyagraha against the injustice done to the workers. Finally the British were compelled to stop their inhuman treatment of the workers. This satyagraha came to be known as the 'Champaranya Satyagraha'.

After the success of the 'Champaranya Satyagraha', Gandhi felt that he should settle down in one place. He selected a site near the banks of the Sabarmati River in Gujarat, and established his Ashram there. He decided that thereafter he would devote all his time to the service of humanity, and work for the downtrodden. He preached what he practiced. He picked up the cause of the Harijans who were treated most atrociously all over the country. He raised his voice against the inhuman and unjust treatment meted out to them. He started two newspapers 'Harijan' and 'Young India', and through them he expressed his views and spread social awareness in the people.

In 1920, Lokmanya Tilak died, and Gandhi became the leader of the Freedom Movement. Under his guidance, the people went on Satyagraha to fight against injustice. He was arrested and imprisoned many times, but that did not deter him and his loyal followers. They continued their fight for freedom with even greater fervour. Gandhi was greatly respected for his simple living, high thinking, and fearless attitude. The British too were greatly impressed by him, and called him for negotiations regarding India's freedom. Since it had been decided that the freedom struggle would not stop until full freedom was granted, the negotiations did not serve any purpose.

Various forms of Satyagraha and Civil Disobedience movements took place at that time. The 'Swadeshi Movement' (to use local made goods) was one of them. Gandhi advised and encouraged the people to use Indian goods and use Khadi (hand spun cloth). He himself wore Khadi clothes, and would sit to spin on his Charkha (Spinning wheel). People stopped buying British made goods. Instead, they lit born fires of these goods. The Government, with the help of the police and the army, tried its best to put an end to all these demonstrations and agitations, but these were unsuccessful. On the contrary, they became more intense. The Government had imposed a tax on salt, and Gandhi started the 'Salt Satyagraha'.

He and many other leaders were imprisoned, but the struggle for freedom continued with greater intensity. While India fought for freedom, in Europe, the second world war had begun. The British looked towards India for help, but Gandhi started the Non-cooperation Movement. Jawaharlal Nehru and many other Indian leaders joined the movement because they all had immense faith in Gandhi. The British Government thought it would please the Indians by granting them partial freedom. Once again they began negotiations with Gandhi, but Gandhi made it clear that he and his people wanted nothing less than complete freedom (Independence). To make this demand stronger, the Indian National Congress passed the Quit India resolution in 1942, wherein they demanded that the British leave India immediately. Angered by this resolution, the British again imprisoned him and his wife Kasturba.

Kasturba died in jail. She was always behind him in his freedom movements and the other leaders. Many secret organizations were formed as a result, and they put a number of obstacles in the regular functioning of the Government. Around this time Netaji Subhashchandra Bose formed his 'Azad Hind Fauj' in Japan. Many Indians who were in the British Army, left it and joined the Indian National Army. The British Government realized that it was now impossible for them to continue their rule in India, they released Gandhi and other leaders from prison, and once again began negotiations with him. Finally, on 15th August 1947, India attained freedom, and for the first time the Indian tri-colour National flag fluttered on the Red Fort in Delhi.

However, in its fight for freedom, India had to pay a heavy price. What was once a large single geographical unit, now comprised of two new nations – India and Pakistan. It was during this period that Hindu-Muslim riots took place all over the country. People of both communities were killed brutally, and there was large scale bloodshed all around. Gandhi put his life in danger, pleaded with the people and made ceaseless efforts to stop this senseless killing. After Independence, Gandhi concentrated his attention on the betterment of the Downtrodden people. He went from village to village and advised the people that for the good of the country it was necessary for everyone to work together in unity and harmony.

Equal opportunities and equal status was what he wanted. Although Gandhi strived so hard for unity, there were some people who were under the misconception that Gandhi favoured the Muslims. On 30th January 1948, in Delhi, when Gandhi set out to attend a prayer meeting, he was shot dead by an assailant. His last words were 'Hey Ram'. People all over the world paid rich tribute to Gandhi. The great Mahatma's life had come to an end! The news shocked everyone.

Not only India, but the whole world mourned the death of the great man ?a real Mahatma, who had dedicated his entire life to the service of humanity, and had taught the importance of truth, brotherhood, peace, non-violence, equality and simplicity. The most befitting tribute that we can pay him is to follow the path he has shown us.

■■■

Inflation in India: Fuelled by Demand?

Recent spurt in prices came as a rude shock to the government which was preparing to take on the serious economic challenges like tumbling of the stock exchanges in the country and global slowdown. In a democratic system like ours, nothing can be more worrying to the party in power than the soaring prices in an election year. Surprisingly, the inflationary pressure is coupled with the reduction in economic growth of the country, and defying the principles of monetary theory, the Indian economy is behaving like a typical developing economy. By the end of March, the inflation rate had reached an alarming 7.41 per cent level and has been hovering above 7 per cent thereafter.

No one need to scratch one's head to find out the reasons for the price rise in the recent weeks, despite several desperate measures taken by the government to control it. First and foremost is the global environment. Globally, the prices of food articles have risen by about 75 per cent during the last about six months. The situation is so precarious in the African continent that groups of people suffering from hunger in several African countries have tried to loot the foodgrain stores of the government and the other organizations.

The world community became even more concerned after the recent report that the world has been left with food stocks only for three to four weeks. Sharad Pawar, the Agriculture Minister of India was quick to respond to the above report and announced that the situation was under control in the country, as the buffer stocks of food were more than the prescribed limit. But notwithstanding the said assertion by the Agriculture Minister, the prices of foodgrains, edible oils, pulses, fruits, vegetables etc. continue to head northwards.

In India, agriculture sector is growing at the rate of around two per cent while the growth rate of population is also around two per cent. In other words, more people in the world are chasing lesser food articles, resulting in pressure on the prices. In addition, the world economy is also trying to pay attention to the sectors having high growth potential and the primary sector is getting ignored. India has not been an exception in this regard.

Global prices of crude oil have been on the rise during the past about two years now. Towards the end of April, the crude oil prices in the international market had crossed $ 120 per gallon, putting pressure on the government to increase the retail prices of petrol and diesel in the country. Increase in the prices of these products has cascading effect on the prices of other commodities due to increase in the transportation cost. This has been one major factors responsible for higher inflation rate in the country.

Another factor responsible for the constant increase in prices has been the rising prices of cement and steel. This is perhaps due to increased demand for steel and cement due to increased construction activity, infrastructure development through various flagship programmes of the government and increased demand for these commodities for such programmes and the activities of the National Highway Authority of India. Increased steel prices put pressure on the prices of many products that use steel as raw material, including the automobiles, construction industry and other such industries.

Defying Monetary Policy?

As per the monetary theory, inflation is largely a monetary phenomenon and it is the monetary policy measures that come to the rescue of the government to control inflation. In developed countries, it is the increased money supply that generally causes inflation and the government takes monetary measures like increasing the bank rate, Credit Reserve Ratio (CRR), increasing the deposit rates to mop up the surplus flow of money in the economy. Traditionally, inflation in India has generally defied the monetary theory and has refused to be curbed by the monetary measures.

The economy has been growing at around 8 per cent per annum during the past five years and the forecast for the current financial year is also around eight per cent. But, on the other hand, the prices of food articles, cement, steel and oil are on the rise. Though the agricultural sector has been growing at slower rate of around 2 per cent per annum, other sectors like the manufacturing and the services sector are booming with a growth rate in double digits. All these factors contradict the teachings of the monetary policy.

Another principle of the monetary policy is that the price rise due to increased money supply of one commodity is offset by the price fall of another. In a poor and agrarian country like ours, where majority of the people spend major chunk of their earnings on food articles, this cannon seems ridiculous. With food scarcities galore and the food prices soaring, it is immoral to say that the increase in the prices of food articles is offset by reduction in the prices of other goods, say cosmetics. People need food at every cost and not the cheaper cosmetics!

The above phenomenon has forced the policy makers to control inflation by moving away from the monetary policy measures to other measures. One of the most frequently used measures has been the changes in the import-export policy. To tackle inflation, India has often resorted to the policy of reducing the import duties on the food articles, on the one hand, and banning the exports of the select food items, on the other.

Recently, Raghuram Rajan Committee had suggested that the Reserve Bank of India should not resort to routine multi-tasking covering the exchange rate, growth and inflation, but should focus primarily on control of inflation. It is believed by many that in the Indian conditions, non-core inflation is often the dominant part of inflation, and under such a scenario, the monetary policy measures are week tools for curbing inflation. The policies which are successful in the European countries may not work in the country like ours and there is no point in blindly following the monetary policy measures as prescribed in the economic (monetary) theory book.

Corrective Actions

The Wholesale Price Index (WPI) is an index of a few commodities and if one looks at the composition of such goods, the prices of several articles have not undergone any change, indicating the inflation rate at 7.41 per cent as on 29th March 2008.

For example, fertilizers and pesticides have about 10 per cent weight in the index, but the prices of these commodities have not undergone any major change in the last one year. But even if these two commodities are excluded, a significant percentage of index representing a host of commodities has remained unchanged over the last several months. Electrical goods, for example represent about 2 per cent weight in the WPI and their prices have remained static during the last about eight months.

The above facts indicate that the WPI takes into account the weighted average of the commodities included by the government in it and ignores the prices of the commodities that are excluded from the index. Hence, in the modern day of consumerism, where there are several segments in a particular commodity, the WPI needs to be made broad based to include more commodities. As on today, it does not represent the true picture about the price rise in the country.

For rural and agricultural workers the impact of the inflation has been even higher. Ironically, these categories have very low income levels when compared to the national average. Consumer Price Index (CPI) for the agricultural labourers and rural labourers during the month of March has been close to 8 per cent. Since the calendar year 2007, the CPI for the agricultural labourers (CPI-AL) has been increasing at a much faster rate than the WPI. During April-March 2007-08, CPI-AL has remained higher than the WPI, with the gap between the two being around 3.5 per cent at an average. The reason is that the CPI has higher weightage for the food and consumer items than the WPI. This also explains why the impact of price rise for the consumer is higher than the announced inflation rate by the government. CPI is more relevant to the consumers and not the WPI.

House rents and miscellaneous services have also

become dearer than before, adding to the worries of the consumers. As per the latest data released by the NSSO, the most consumed items in the Indian households are rice, wheat, onion, potato, milk, arhar and edible oils. During April-March 2007-08, the WPI of rice increased by 6.35 per cent, arhar by 14.52 per cent, milk by 8.68 per cent, wheat by 5.57 per cent, mustard oil by 28.91 per cent and coconut oil by 10.8 per cent.

Increased prices of the food articles are attributed to the supply side constraints and the developments in the international markets. Exports have become expensive due to the global price rise. Hence, the government was left with no alternative but to take measures to control inflation directly. The zero import duty facility has been extended to the import of several food commodities and export of pulses has been completely banned. Further, several State governments like Delhi and Maharashtra initiated several de-hoarding drives by raiding the foodgrain godowns.

Being in the election year, the UPA government at the Centre can ill-afford to let the situation of price rise prevail and perpetuate. The measures have begun to show some results when the inflation rate eased to 7.14 per cent during the week ending April 5, 2008. It is felt that a spell of good monsoons would further improve the position, while the failure of the monsoons may spell doom not only for the farmers, but also for the consumers.

■■■

How to Plan your Career?

Choosing a career is a difficult matter, in the best of times. Add to this opinions of friends and parents, and the young person is caught up in a confusing situation where making a decision is almost impossible. We give here a model which can help young people to choose a career, gain competencies required for it, make decisions, set goals and take action. The decision for each individual is different, since everyone is a distinct individual. This model is helpful not only for freshers but also throughout one's life.

Self-Assessment

This step involves gathering information about yourself to make a decision about a career. By developing an understanding of self (values, interests, aptitudes, abilities, personal traits, and desired life style) you should become aware of the inter-relationship between self and occupational choice.

One can start by *(a)* Learning interests, abilities, skills, and work values, *(b)* Listing accomplishments, *(c)* Understanding physical and psychological needs, *(d)* Assessing aspirations and motivation level, and *(e)* Deciphering personal traits and characteristics.

As you begin to develop a better understanding of yourself, you will gain self-awareness, improve self-confidence, understand the importance of time management and also develop personal as well as professional management skills.

Some ways in which self-assessment can be done are

described here. For example, one can take exploratory classes or attend workshops for study skills, or join activity clubs or professional clubs. One must be careful that one should allow regular time for leisure, hobbies and friends and not get involved in work all the time.

One should identify one's personality style and see what one is best suited to. Also identify work values and gain a positive attitude.

For instance, one should develop interpersonal skills in expressing feelings and ideas and interact with people. Self-defeating behaviour should be got over with.

Academic and Career Options

After you have completed your self-assessment, you must identify academic and career options available. This step allows you to investigate the world of work, narrow a general occupational direction into a specific one through an informed decision-making process. You will begin to identify potential careers, gather information about those careers, and match the career information with the results from your self-assessment.

Once this is done, one should learn about academic and career entrance requirements. Explore how and where you can get the education and training required. Identify institutes where you want to apply. Also assess job market trends and have a second plan ready, consisting of academic and career alternatives.

Competency Areas

It is important to improve competency all the times. One must gain research and investigative skills, practice decision-making, develop problem-solving skills and take up critical thinking exercises.

One must also increase understanding of how abilities, interests, and values match career/academic requirements.

To gain competency, one should interact with professionals, meet academic advisors and career counsellors, discuss with professors, or attend courses and workshops in areas where one can learn skills. Skills that can be thus acquired are: communications, computer knowledge, foreign languages and international studies. A youngster must make it a point to attend job and career fairs, participate in the Study Abroad programme, or take up a part-time job. Students abroad are known to start small businesses in order to enhance their skills.

The next step helps you to evaluate occupational choices and gain practical experience through internships, co-operative education, summer jobs, volunteer work and campus activities. You will begin to make more specific decisions about occupational choices. Here too, increase your competency levels by learning communication and interpersonal skills. Confidence-building is very important at this stage. Time management techniques should also be picked up.

At this stage too, one should participate in the Alumni programmes of your college, work part-time or during summer to acquire new skills and practice public-speaking in classes or in organizations, tutor students in various subjects, or join a professional organization.

Meet Professionals

Now start finding out about your occupational prospects. Find out about the major duties and responsibilities involved, products made or services provided by this occupation, specialisation within the occupation and the tools used in the occupation. Find out also about the education, training or experience needed for the occupation. Match personal qualifications, skills, and abilities required for the occupation and fill in the gaps where you do not have such skills, such as typing or computer knowledge.

Assess whether you like the working conditions: some jobs may require odd hours of duty or frequent travel. Are you up to facing these? Find out about future prospects and outlook for the occupation. The normal methods of entry into the occupation will be found in newspapers and magazines. Observe the people in the occupation and see the personality characteristics of typical people working in it. Sales jobs, for example, require extroverts and you should be able to match your personality with what you observe.

Make an informational interview questionnaire and talk to people in the occupation. The following questions could act as a guide:

a) How did you get into this occupation/organization?

b) How did you become interested in this occupation/organization?

c) What entry-level jobs might qualify a person for this field?

d) What is the progression of jobs from the beginning to the top?

e) What responsibilities and duties do you have in your work?

f) Who are your customers? Who are your competitors?

g) What essential abilities are needed to do your job well?

h) What preparation, education, training, or background is required entrance into this field of work?

i) What is the guiding philosophy of the organization?

j) What personal traits, values, and interests are necessary or to succeed and advance in this occupation/organization?

k) What are the major frustrations, annoyances, or sources of in the occupation/organization?

l) How much time do you spend at work?

Meeting professionals helps a lot and clarifies many doubts in one's mind. However, it is necessary to know someone for honest answes. If you do not know a person, chances are that you will not be able to get honest answers.

Matching Skills with Requirements

The basic idea of the above model is to match one's skills with what is required for the job. Once an assessment is made, one will be better able to know one's personality and choose a career accordingly. Very often, this is not done. Thus, people find themselves in jobs in which they have no interest in. A person who has been involved in books all his life, is suddenly asked to deal with customers or a person who has been an extrovert may find himself in a banking job where all he has to do is keep ledgers. It is to avoid this kind of a thing that building inventory helps.

At the same time, the model helps you assess the skills needed to work in certain careers. If you want to do management, for example, it is advisable to take up jobs so that one acquires confidence and also knowledge about the industry. This will also help in selecting the kind of industry that you want to work in. The model is not perfect, but gives invaluable pointers about one's personality and indicates how to choose a career.

■ ■ ■

Emergence of New Words, Idioms in the Language

How certain words get universal acceptance, others get rejected, some of them gain currency, others fall into disuse—the phenomenon remains complex and escapes full understanding. From common experience we know that even old words re-emerge with new meanings and get loaded with new significance. For example, take the Hindustani word *chamcha* that we knew three or four decades ago as merely a "spoon". But we do not know how and when this word *chamcha* re-emerged with new meanings and significance and became an inevitable part of gossip and even serious talk or writing. *Chamcha* and *Chamchi* now signify not a small ladle to scoop food from a dish or a piece of cutlery but a lackey—some one who flatters and servilely goes about doing errands for a more important person.

Any living language or speech continues throwing up new words, idioms or lexicon units in the form of phrases or sentences or sayings or proverbs. This is how a lexicon continues to grow and enrich itself. We now have dictionaries and professional outfits to keep a watch on new words and coinages but the language has been growing for centuries and adding words to its domain uninterruptedly.

Medical and scientific terms are created by specialists; so also is the case with various other branches of knowledge. But here we are concerned with the phenomenon of words emerging from common speech and then acquiring a distinct existence and place in the commonly accepted usage.

Perhaps language developed after Man acquired the ability to form words and felt the need to name objects—though we can only speculate about such things. We can also presume that in the beginning naming things and objects was a simple affair, as one word stood for one particular object or thing.

Though we depend on language to say things logically, the way a language develops is hardly logical. For example, why is a spoon called a spoon? We have no logical answer to this question. The process of word formation and their acceptance becomes even more complex and mysterious when we move from objects to thoughts and ideas and concepts. Abstract notions cannot be directly perceived through our senses yet through language we are able to express and communicate thoughts, ideas and concepts among ourselves and even from generation to generation.

We may have different understanding or definitions of Justice, Liberty and Equality but early in life we begin to understand what they stand for in our cultural and social environment. Such words develop their meaning through time and social space and even keep changing their meanings in the changing contexts.

Thus, we cannot say precisely how a language develops and then ceases to be spoken and written as did the classical languages like Sanskrit, Pali, Latin and Greek.

Currently, much interest centres on new words, idioms and lexical units that have been entering the English language in recent times.

"Did you eat a *balti* before 1984 or have a *mullet* before 1994? And do you know how they got their names?" asks Robert Faber of the Oxford English Dictionary (OED). The OED now openly invites you to hunt for words and help rewrite 'the greatest book in the English language'. The internet has made the task of word hunting easier in our own times. It was not so always.

Dr Johnson, credited with writing/compiling the first English Dictionary 250 years ago had to depend upon just six helpers or assistants.

Now the BBC and the Oxford English Dictionary, with their enormous, world-wide resources, have teamed up and appealed to users of the English language everywhere to help solve "some of the most intriguing recent word mysteries in the language".

The OED has sought to "find the earliest verifiable usage of every single word in the English language—currently 600,000 in the OED and counting—and of every separate meaning of every word. Quite a task!"

The OED's BBC Wordhunt appeal listed fifty words/phrases and dated them for their entry into the English language. They also challenged all those who cared to respond to bring up evidence to prove the OED dates of entry wrong.

Some of the words/phrases in their list are: balti, Beeb, boffin, codswallop, full monty, mushy peas, pear-shaped, and pop one's clogs.

It also defies logic how some words are short and others are long. The longest words in the OED is: 'pneumonoultramicroscopicsilicovolcanoconiosis', that according to it is a factitious word alleged to mean 'a lung disease caused by the inhalation of very fine silica dust' (but occurring chiefly as an instance of a very long word!)

While we do not know how new words/phrases/lexical units actually get into the English language, it is a solace to know that the OED Editors are prepared to tell us how they draft them for entry into the Oxford English Dictionary.

Graeme Diamond, a member of the team responsible for recording and drafting new words for the Oxford English Dictionary, explains the process of how a word appearing in your newspaper finds its way into the OED:

"Imagine that you are reading your favourite newspaper over breakfast. The news column tells you that new "e-tailers" have underestimated the time it takes to build a loyal customer base. You discover that the term is an abbreviation of "electronic retailer".

It is very likely that this word will have been picked up by the OED's Reading Programme, a large ongoing project employing around fifty readers.

All types of contemporary printed material are looked at—novels, television scripts, song lyrics, and so on, as well as newspapers and magazines—and searched for entirely new words, or interesting new uses of existing words. The findings of the Reading Programme are stored in a vast searchable electronic database of quotation material called 'Incomings'.

In one of my regular analyses of the Incomings database, I see that "e-tailer" has appeared several times in recent publications. I note the word for further investigation, and perhaps for eventual inclusion in the Dictionary."

"A rule of thumb is that any word can be included which appears five times, in five different printed sources, over a period of five years", informs Graeme Diamond.

A few new words, idioms, lexical units to enter most recently published Concise Oxford English Dictionary (Revised Eleventh Edition) are:

Abdominoplasty—A surgical operation involving the removal of excess flesh from the abdomen.

Agroterrorism—Terrorist acts intended to disrupt or damage a country's agriculture.

Bahookie—Scottish a person's buttocks.

The elephant in the room—A phrase meaning a major problem or controversial issue but avoided as it is more comfortable to do so.

Hoody (also hoodie)—A person, especially a youth, wearing a hooded top.

Retronym—A new term created from an existing word.

Shoulder-surfing—The practice of spying on the user of a cash-dispensing machine.

Twonk—A stupid or foolish person.

Yogalates—A fitness routine that combines Pilates exercises with yoga postures.

Zombie—A computer controlled by a hacker without the owner's knowledge.

Idioms have acquired greater importance due to the increased interest in second language learning. An idiom is a phrase where the words together have a meaning that is different from the dictionary definitions of the individual words, which can make idioms hard for English As A Second Language learners to understand. Idiomatic expressions are peculiar to a culture and until one is immersed in the second language's culture they may not carry much meaning.

For instance, "A day late and a dollar short" cannot be grasped through dictionary meanings of individual words. Interaction with American environment will help understand the idiom which suggests that "if something is a day late and a dollar short, it is too little, too late."

Likewise, 'A penny for your thoughts' will require knowledge of the British environment as "this idiom is used as a way of asking someone what they are thinking about".

In the beginning was the Word, and the Word was God, says the Bible. *Akshra* is indestructible, say the Hindu classics. New words are then like *Avatars*.

■ ■ ■

The Retailing Scenario in India

According to a UN report on the state of world population, by 2008 close to 3.3 billion people had shifted to cities and almost 5 billion will shift by 2030. The next few decades will see an unprecedented urban growth in the developing world, notably in Africa and Asia. By 2030, the towns and cities of the developing world will make up 80 per cent of urban humanity. This urbanization trend provides both a setting and a perspective for reviewing the emerging retail juggernaut on the Indian scene. For, growth of organized retail is predominantly an urban phenomenon.

The prospects of organized retail are determined by the level of urban population. Analysts suggest that urban families spend 2.5 times more than rural families. In India, urban population is growing at a CAGR (cumulative annual growth rate) of 2.4% annually. India will, thus, have an urbanization of 30%, increasing to 32% by 2015. In Brazil, one of the BRIC economies, urbanization level is 85%. The Brazil organized retail has a 36% market share of total retail.

In China, organized retail has a 20% market share of total retail, with 42% urbanization level.

Skeptics point out that India does not have China's booming manufacturing sector that helped Chinese rapid urbanization. Manufacturing sector creates urban centres whereas service sector comes later to service the urban centres. India currently has service sector dominance.

(1) Chandigarh, (2) Nagpur, (3) Goa, Kochi, (4)

Visakhapatnam, (5) Ahmedabad, (6) Bhubaneswar, (7) Jaipur, (8) Mysore, (9) Indore, (10) Lucknow, (11) Coimbatore, (12) Guwahati, (13) Ludhiana, (14) Surat, are the fastest growing cities of India and organized retail is likely to target these and growing towns neighbouring mega-cities.

We must know that organized retail is yet another aspect of global shift from industrial to knowledge society. Retail selling has been there since the very beginnings of organized society but the change from individual shop to malls or mega stores is recent.

In China and India, its scale appears overwhelming because of the threatened displacement of traditional shopping structure that needed no special knowledge or training. Nor was competition so visibly challenging. These new retail mega bazaars will need trained sales and space management staff. Organized retailing is, thus, more than a matter of size and scale.

India has the highest number of shops in the world— 11 shops for every 1000 persons—but Indian *kiryana* shops are not the so-called mom-n-pop stores of the west. They may be spared the fate that small shops in western countries have met at the hands of organized retail. The key factor is the role of population density.

A cursory survey will show that in a country with considerable area (say more than 500,000 sq km), organized retail flourishes when population density is low. USA has a population density of 31 person per sq km. Brazil has a density of 21 person per sq km. European Union has a population density of 112 people per sq km. Even China with a population much more than India has a density of 135 people per sq km. In India it is 332 persons per sq km!

Besides density of population, another factor to be considered is the diversity of population. India is peculiar and very different from any other country and nation. It is not only a multilingual and multicultural country but a country of vast difference in taste for food, clothing and colour and consumption preference. Chain store system works on the principle of uniformity.

It is the cultural pockets within India that dictate the Indian consumer behaviour. Also, the sharp regional disparities are a veritable impediment to uniform supply of consumer goods and are likely to slow down or blunt the edge of retail onslaught. What sells in Tamil Nadu may not sell in Punjab.

Even within a region, what sells in Mumbai may not sell in Nagpur. Even within the city like Mumbai, what works in Malabar Hills may not work in Borivilli or Dahisar.

Organized retail is a game of standardization. It is a game of mass scale selling where everything is so standardized as to squeeze the supplier to submit to the lowest possible price.

In India, standardization is a challenge. Indians defy standardization. One can see this by merely travelling on the road. If you observe the standard rules of the road, you are bound to meet with an accident. Each one for oneself.

This has something to do with our philosophy of life. One realizes oneself not because of society, but in spite of society and others. Each Indian has his deity and his own way of pleasing his gods. We do not like to reach a function, meeting or even office at the given time. We like to set our own time. In market terminology we are a "nation of customization".

To help stay as customers rather than consumers, there are the market imitators who can copy goods and sell so-called "duplicates" or fakes at much lower prices.

And the consumer has no complaints if he gets a fake for fifty rupees of the original costing five hundred rupees. The fake or duplicate often proves better than the original as every car or scooter owner knows. Here standard things don't work.

Take a typical household in India. How happy is an average Indian housewife while rattling off the list of customization of morning break-fast of her family—the son wants toast, butter, and double-egg omelet; daughter wants corn flakes with honey; hubby wants *aalu paratha* with decent helpings and *dahi* (curd), and she herself prefers the leftovers, perhaps.

We want everything our way. Not the retailers way. Here, a friendly *kiryana* store has a clear advantage.

But then, times are changing. All we can say is that the *kiryana* store and his delivery boy are going to be around for a while because, in this blessed country, there is room for all kinds. Slacks, jeans as well as salwars will co-exist.

The new-fanged retailers will have to be inventive with their packaging. The Indians are not yet ready for King Size or Economy Size bottles and packets. Indians are tentative buyers and prefer small, "homoeopathic" dozes. Look at the large-scale selling of shampoos and biscuits.

It is the sachet and the small pack that sells the most. "Until sachet happened, .. shampoo was considered a luxury by majority of Indians. A typical Indian doesn't have money to indulge in bulk purchases", says a keen observer of Indian consumer behaviour.

Now look at average American couple who buys six months of toilet paper whenever Wal-mart comes up with a great offer and have a separate storage room in their house to keep discounted and advanced purchases! How many average Indian householders can afford this type of shopping?

Growth of organized retail depends on volumes of selling as well as buying. Sachet economy may not be enough to sustain organized retail. *Kiryana* shops are better placed to service a sachet economy. *Kiryana* stores will rule India for a long time.

Going by the growth rate of total retail and rate of urbanization, urban market in top 1000 cities/towns is likely to double in size to $200 billion by 2015. That means Organized Retail will have to capture 32% of the urban market to meet the projected $64 billion of organized retail revenue by 2015.

In view of near monopoly of *kiryana* in 95% of these top 1000 towns, coupled with poor infrastructure, it will not be easy to attain.

Success of organized retail also depends on supplier capacity to deliver large volumes of standardized product quality at competitive prices. India has thousands of small manufacturers of consumer goods, but few capable of servicing hyper-marts.

India's agricultural land holdings too are high

fragmented, average size being less than a hectare. It would take thousands of such holdings to service a big retailer. Soon, too many retailers may be chasing too few quality agricultural suppliers, disarraying economies of scale.

Inconsistent quality and specification will cause other problems. Contract farming is a possible solution but is in infancy presently.

So far the focus of retail players is on front-end buying of real estate at exorbitant prices, attracting customers to the glitzy malls, but the backbone of Retail is back-end operations—storage, cold chain facilities, road and air connectivity that are slower and need massive investment.

Current retail and fun-filled shopping experience is confined to 6% of India's population in top six cities, contributing 14% of India's GDP and accounting for 68% of organized retail. Going beyond this will be slower, tough and less glamorous.

■■■

Rise of Entrepreneurs in India

There is a galore of Indian entrepreneurs in the Forbes' list of the world's wealthiest every year. But, this is merely a factoid; more significant is the rise of new entrepreneurs in India. In almost every new industry that has attained stature in the last decade, the rising star is not from the established business houses but an upstart.

Take Sunil Mittal, whose phone company now has the sixth-highest value. Ten years back, Mittal would not have figured even in the B list of Indian businessmen. Today, he is ahead not only of patricians like Tatas but also of a global major like Hutchison-Whampoa.

Naresh Goyal's Jet Aiways, barely in fifteen years, has emerged as the largest airline in the country, upstaging the State-owned Indian Airlines, and buying up a private sector rival, Sahara.

In the sunrise retailing sector the big boys, Kishore Biyani and B.S. Nagesh, are creating a furore. Kishore, a totally unknown name a decade ago is now a media darling, a man-on-the-go. Pantaloon and Shoppers' Stop are the Indian challengers-in-waiting for Wal-Mart as they have already swept the likes of Tata (Trent) and RPG off the floor in the retail business.

What about the country's leading airports? The carpetbaggers here are again first-generation names like G.M. Rao and G.V.K. Reddy. Having interesting histories in banking, power and hoteliering, both are now into the big league after outdoing airport bids against celebrities with household surnames.

The most extraordinary stories of meteoric rise in the annals of entrepreneurship, however, belong to Narayana Murthy, Azim Premji and Shiv Nadar. They have surpassed their counterparts in advanced countries in software development and helped India emerge as the leading Software power. In the same breath, we must mention Subhash Chandra, the amusement parks owner and a pioneer of satellite TV in India. Within a few years he has outperformed the oldest media house in the country.

Uday Kotak has founded a bank that promises to be yet another ICICI. Rajeev Chandrashekhar, an engineer-turned-telecom tycoon is truly an adventurer. Returning from the US, he got into a telecom business, sold it out and is now entering into freight transport —as the railways are privatising the container business. Kiran Mazumdar Shaw, another pioneer, has made impressive forays into biotech industry.

Among the electronic media enterprisers Prannoy Roy and Raghav Behl are India's news kings. How about Jignesh Shah, the challenger. He is another first-generation business entrepreneur involved in a David-Goliath duel with the country's biggest financial players for market leadership in commodity exchange. The list is getting longer daily.

Only a few decades back, Indian entrepreneurs had to leave India in order to prove their spirit of enterprise. Aditya Birla wandered all over South-East Asia setting up companies and factories. Laxmi Mittal had to flee his homeland to become the world's steel sultan.

Doing business in India is no cakewalk, what with the bureaucracy's red tape and greasy palms, yet the Indian entrepreneur is proving his mettle. India is now a vast and vibrant market. Capital can be organized and technology accessed. De-regulation is creating new opportunities. Forbes list is no longer an Everest for Indian entrepreneurs.

Indian business is also fanning out and challenging the global multinationals. For instance, Tata is now one of the world's lowest-cost steel producers. Indians are shaking Europe, America, other continents with their global mega-mergers and hostile takeovers. L.N. Mittal—based in London but holding an Indian passport—grabbed the world's largest steel-maker, Arcelor. Tata, not to be left behind, gobbled up another major steel manufacturer, Corus, to become the fifth largest producer. These deals hail the emergence of global Indian entrepreneurs on the world stage. India is fast becoming a hub for metals, petro-products and auto components.

India's second largest private firm, the Mukesh Ambani-owned Reliance Industries, may soon be among the top 10 in the world list.

According to a Boston Consulting Group (BCG) report, "a revolution in global business is under way", and the axis of corporate power was shifting towards the BRIC (Brazil, Russia, India and China) countries.

A 2006 study by Mape, an investment bank, observed: "the Indian Multinational Company (MNC) has finally come of age" and "Indian buyers have become a force to reckon with in many industries such as pharma, auto components and oil and gas". Liberal policies, access to cash, and the rise of entrepreneurial ambitions are creating conditions for the emergence of global Indian enterprises.

Besides the exceptional first-timer Indira Nooyi, the Pepsico chief, many banks, insurance companies and business enterprises now have women in key positions—chief executives, chief strategists, chief economists. Many head the human resource wings and are tough and tactful while dealing with the hard-core politicos and burly men dominating the restive trade unions. Kiran Shaw Majumdar, Biocon chief, or Anu Agha, who took over Thermax after her husband's sudden death, is no transient phenomenon but is becoming a normal face of Indian business.

Higher education and new confidence are helping daughters and daughters-in-law of traditional families take up high-profile corporate roles. Women are better students, quick to grasp the nitty-gritty of work and more willing to listen to elders.

Shefali Munjal is a third generation member of the Munjal family who manages Hero Group, among the world's largest two-wheeler makers.

Priya and Priti Paul of Apeejay Surrendra Group, met the challenge after their father got killed in a terrorist attack in India's turbulent northeast, where the family has a tea business.

Sulajja Firodia Motwani manages her Kinetic Group as well as family. She joined the family enterprise on returning from Carnegie Mellon University. Mallika Srinivasan of Chennai-based Tractor and Farm Equipment is the eldest daughter of A. Sivasailam, chairman of the Rs 25 billion Amalgamations Group, and wife of Venu Srinivasan of the TVS Group. She is rated as one of the most successful Indian women CEOs.

Cremica is a popular biscuit and confectionery brand where Geeta Bector is both director and wife of Akshay Bector, M.D. She thinks women have a special advantage when it comes to food.

S.K. Dhamija in his book *Women Entrepreneurs* says: "The hidden entrepreneurial potentials of women have gradually been changing with the growing sensitivity to the role and economic status in society... Today, women entrepreneurs represent a group that has broken away from the beaten track and are exploring new avenues of economic participation." It is estimated that women entrepreneurs currently comprise about 10 per cent of the total number of entrepreneurs in India.

Shashi Ruia describes his Essar Group as "serial entrepreneurs" and predicts the rise of new entrepreneurs. "There has not been a better time in India to reach out and touch the horizon ... entrepreneurship is no more limited to family-managed businesses in India", he said while addressing a Convocation of the Entrepreneurship Institute of India.

■■■

Global Tobacco Epidemic

100 million dead in the 20th century. Currently 5.4 million deaths every year. Unless urgent action is taken: By 2030, there will be more than 8 million deaths every year. By 2030, more than 80% of tobacco deaths will be in developing countries. One billion estimated deaths predicted during the 21st century.

The above statistics are scary, indeed. "Reversing this entirely preventable epidemic must now rank as a top priority for public health and for political leaders in every country of the world," according to Dr Margaret Chan, WHO Director-General.

Tobacco is the only legal consumer product that can harm everyone exposed to it–and it kills up to half of those who use it as intended. Yet, tobacco use is common throughout the world due to low prices, aggressive and widespread marketing, lack of awareness about its dangers, and inconsistent public policies against its use.

Most of tobacco's damage to health does not become evident until years or even decades after the onset of use. So, while tobacco use is rising globally, the epidemic of tobacco-related disease and death has just begun.

The global consensus that we must fight the tobacco epidemic has already been established by more than 150 Parties to the WHO Framework Convention on Tobacco Control.

Now, the WHO Report on the Global Tobacco Epidemic gives countries a roadmap that builds on the WHO Framework Convention to turn this global consensus into a global reality through MPOWER, a package of six effective tobacco control policies.

To support MPOWER, WHO and its global partners are providing new resources to help countries stop the disease, death and economic damage caused by tobacco use. When implemented and enforced as a package, the six policies will prevent young people from beginning to smoke, help current smokers quit, protect non-smokers from exposure to second-hand smoke and free countries and their people from tobacco's harm.

Economics of Tobacco

Although the tobacco industry claims it creates jobs and generates revenues that enhance local and national economies, the industry's overriding contribution to any country is suffering, disease, death – and economic losses. Tobacco use currently costs the world hundreds of billions of dollars each year.

The net economic effect of tobacco is to deepen poverty. The industry's business objective – to get more customers addicted – disproportionately hurts the poor. Tobacco use is higher among the poor than the rich in most countries, and the difference in tobacco use between poor and rich is greatest in regions where average income is among the lowest.

For the poor, money spent on tobacco means money not spent on basic necessities such as food, shelter, education and health care. The poorest households in Bangladesh spend almost 10 times as much on tobacco as on education. In Indonesia, where smoking is most common among the poor, the lowest income group spends 15% of its total expenditure on tobacco. In Egypt, more than 10% of household expenditure in low-income homes is on tobacco. The poorest 20% of households in Mexico spend nearly 11% of their household income on tobacco. Medical costs from smoking impoverish more than 50 million people in China.

The poor are much more likely than the rich to become ill and die prematurely from tobacco-related illnesses. This creates greater economic hardship and perpetuates the circle of poverty and illness. Early deaths of primary wage earners are especially catastrophic for poor families and communities. When, for example, a 45-year-old Bangladeshi man who heads a low-income household dies of cancer from a 35-year *bidi* habit, the survival of his entire family is at stake. His lost economic capacity is magnified as his spouse, children and other dependants sink deeper into poverty and government or extended family members must take on their support.

Helping the Addicts

People who are addicted to nicotine are victims of the tobacco epidemic. Among smokers who are aware of the dangers of tobacco, three out of four want to quit. Like people dependent on any addictive drug, it is difficult for most tobacco users to quit on their own and they benefit from help and support to overcome their dependence.

Countries' health-care systems hold the primary responsibility for treating tobacco dependence. Treatment includes various methods, from simple medical advice to pharmaco-therapy, along with telephone help lines known as quit lines, and counselling. These treatment methods have differing cost efficiencies, and do not have a uniform impact on individual tobacco users. Treatment should be adapted to local conditions and cultures, and tailored to individual preferences and needs.

In most cases, a few basic treatment interventions can help tobacco users who want to quit. Three types of treatment should be included in any tobacco prevention effort: *(i)* tobacco cessation advice incorporated into primary health-care services; *(ii)* easily accessible and free quit lines; and *(iii)* access to low-cost pharmacological therapy.

Integrating tobacco cessation into primary health care and other routine medical visits provides the health-care system with opportunities to remind users that tobacco harms their health and that of others around them. Repeated advice at every medical visit reinforces the need to stop using tobacco.

Nicotine replacement therapy reduces withdrawal symptoms by substituting for some of the nicotine absorbed from tobacco. Bupropion, an anti-depressant, can reduce craving and other negative sensations when tobacco users cut back or stop their nicotine intake. Varenicline attaches to nicotine receptors in the brain to prevent the release of dopamine, thus blocking the sensations of pleasure that people can experience when they smoke.

Pharmacological therapy is generally more expensive and considered to be less cost effective than physician advice and quit lines, but it has been shown to double or triple quit rates.

Cessation programmes provide a significant political advantage by enabling governments to help those most directly affected by the epidemic at the same time that they are enacting new restrictions on tobacco. They generally encounter few political obstacles and help foster a national policy of opposition to tobacco use, an important step in creating a tobacco-free society. Governments can use some tobacco tax revenues to help users free themselves from addiction.

Conclusion

In summary, only around 5% of the world's population is covered by any one of the key interventions of effective advertising, promotion and sponsorship bans, smoke-free spaces, prominent pack warnings, protection from deceptive and misleading advertising, promotion and sponsorship, and cessation support. Governments collect more than US$ 200 billion in tobacco tax revenues and have the financial resources to expand and strengthen tobacco control programmes. Further tobacco tax increases can provide additional funding for these initiatives.

The number of people killed each year by tobacco will double over the next few decades unless urgent action is taken. But just as the epidemic of tobacco-caused disease is man-made, people – acting through their governments and civil society – can reverse the epidemic.

Tobacco is unique among today's leading public health problems in that the means to curb the epidemic are clear and within our reach. If countries have the political commitment and technical and logistic support to implement the MPOWER policy package, they can save millions of lives.

Because the tobacco industry is far better funded and more politically powerful than those who advocate to protect children and non-smokers from tobacco and to help tobacco users quit, much more needs to be done by every country to reverse the tobacco epidemic. Unless urgent action is taken, more than one billion people could be killed by tobacco during this century.

■■■

Child Labour

According to the 1991 Census, the number of working children in the country was of the order of 11.28 million. The existence of child labour in hazardous industries continues to be a great problem in India. Non-availability of accurate, authentic and up-to-date data on child labour has been major handicap in planned intervention for eradication of this social evil. However, efforts are underway to modify and improve the existing National Child Labour Project. A major activity undertaken under this scheme is the establishment of special schools to provide non-formal education, vocational training, supplementary nutrition, stipends, health care, etc. to children withdrawn from employment in hazardous industries.

However, this is not a problem that can be solved merely by legislation. Again, a socio-economic problem with deeper roots into the socio-economic strata of the backward states of India (particularly the Bimaru states), child labour is said to be only the symptom of the larger problem – the prevailing inequality in rural Indian society, particularly these states of the country.

Recently, hundreds of children were freed after action by the Mumbai police and some NGOs from zari factories in Mumbai city. Zari work (fine decorative embroidery crafted by hand) calls for delicate, small and nimble fingers, and hence child labourers are often recruited from the poorer areas of the country. Uneducated and often compelled by their poor parents and relatives, these children are transported to the big cities by unscrupulous middlemen who sell them to factory owners. Investigations by NGOs revealed that these kids were malnourished and worked for more than 12 hours a day, often without seeing the outside world for days on stretch. Such inhuman conditions left the children malnourished and in some extreme cases, partially blind (zari work is also a strain in the eyes, compounded by poor light and ventilation in these factories).

It is to be noted that even after the rescue, many children chose to stay back, citing starvation and abject poverty back home as less preferable to the inhuman conditions at these factories. Such is the condition of the child labourer in India.

Contract Labour

The subject of contract labour has generated much heated debate in the economic and industrial circles in India.

For a poor, uneducated and marginalized Indian labourer, contract labour is often better than none at all. However, the labourer often signs himself off to life-long penury with little hope for advancement and improvement of conditions.

However, for an industry or a business, the legalities involved in contract labour (particularly with reference to the Industrial Disputes Act, 1947) disable them to lay-off labourers, solve labour related issues, or even close down unprofitable ventures. In a greater economic scenario, this has caused the Indian textile industry huge losses – and has let countries like China, Pakistan and even Bangladesh ahead.

Bonded Labour

Despite the ban on Bonded Labour through the Bonded Labour System (Abolition) Act, 1976 and the presence of a well-organized government structure to fight it, Bonded Labour is a painful reality in the Indian Economy.

The root cause can be attributed to the ancient caste system or the feudal zamindar system which has existed in India since ancient times. In the Indian psyche, bonded labour has not provoked the same fervour that led to the abolition of slavery in other parts of the world.

Usually, women and children are the victims of bonded labour. According to Human Rights Watch, nearly 60 to 115 million children are victims of bonded labour. Many of these children work in the fields, or in hazardous industries like firecrackers and matchsticks and under poorly supervised conditions.

Often, children are "sold" by their parents or relatives to work to write off a debt which the parent or guardian owes the creditor-labourer. However, this debt never gets paid off – the lack of education of the generations of labourers ensures that – and the master-labourer relationship continues for a long time – in many cases (quoted by the NGO Human Rights Watch), for generations.

■ ■ ■

Labour Issues in India – Brief Overview

For many industries, lack of trained labour force is a problem. However, these problems are compounded by the fact that there are multitudes of unemployed potential labourers who, however, do not have the adequate skills for the job. Additionally, many do not also have the means to market themselves, or to make themselves available for jobs. Hence, lack of availability of labour is not merely a demand-supply problem, it has deeper socio-economic roots that need to be looked at from various perspectives.

However, in many organized sectors where the demand for labour has been effectively met, absenteeism and huge turnover of labourers bring about their own problems. In many cases, absenteeism is prevalent in PSUs and government owned organizations. Causes are many, and include unionism, lack of ownership and participation, availability of alternate employment, misuse of benefits and remuneration and sometimes, lack of effective management control.

Women Employee Problems

Since time immemorial and despite the vast cultural and historical richness of our country, women are still considered less capable than men where labour is concerned. Of course, the reasons are cultural and socio-economic. Firstly, women are not considered physically fit for labour, and are often relegated to menial tasks. This deprives them of adequate compensation. Secondly, physical activity continues beyond working hours, in the household, depriving them of rest. A sacrificial mindset

Labour Issues in India – Brief Overview

also makes them susceptible to malnutrition and poor health, which again affects their livelihood. Therefore, it is hard for women to actually come out of this vicious cycle in which they are trapped, simply because of their gender. The challenge is to change the mindset of a society which still sees women labourers more as beasts of burden.

However, there has been some progress which has been achieved with active government and NGO intervention. In many established companies and industries in the private sector, gender is not a consideration for employment and is neither are women employees and labourers discriminated against for pay or opportunity. In fact, in socially aware business houses like the Tatas, gender equality is an important part of their triple-bottom line concept, which enshrines equal opportunity for all, irrespective of caste, creed, gender, religion, nationality or ethnicity.

Despite these minor but significant positive stories, women continue to receive an unequal deal in the labour sector.

■ ■ ■

India's Foreign Policy: Its Twists and Turns

In 1947, India emerged as the largest democracy in the world. It, however, lacked the matching military and economic power. Since then it has fully participated in international politics, adhering to the letter and spirit of international treaties, conventions and protocols. India substituted word power for effective power to vie with the world powers. The tactic worked, at times poorly, when popular and maximum leaders like Jawaharlal Nehru and Indira Gandhi were the Prime Ministers.

Under their rule, India's foreign policy was more for internal consumption than for impacting on the international order. They could afford to make errors and yet have their way. But costs were heavy for the nation. India had to bear dire consequences for some of their foreign policy errors of judgement, because they placed trust not in India's friends, but in its antagonists.

Currently, India is militarily and economically a stronger country, though it has weaker and minimum leaders. But happily, and perhaps compulsively, our Foreign Policy under Dr. Manmohan Singh's rule is more pragmatic and in tune with the times and practices of the so-called international community.

China's rise as the Super-Asian military and economic power and India's own increasing military and economic power are equally important developments of recent years.

"The US, China and India, along with Japan and Russia, constitute the pentagonal power complex of the

21st century; all of them are acknowledged nuclear weapon powers.

Europe is no longer the focus of international power politics, as it was in the twentieth century. At the very onset of the twenty-first century, it has shifted to Asia and promises to stay there in the foreseeable future.

The USA has recognized India as a responsible nuclear weapon power. It is in USA's long-term interests to see India as a strong and stabilizing power in its region. Therefore, it feels persuaded to assist India in enlarging its global role. Can or should India shun Washington's overtures?

India's changed stature does not permit it to blame others for its own diplomatic errors or justify them on moral grounds. It has itself to decide how far, fast or slow, it wishes to develop its relations with USA and other countries, and on what terms. China, only three decades ago, was a sworn enemy of USA, but now it is USA's most dynamic trade partner. China, in fact, has become a world economic, and consequently a world military power, with the American support. Yet, China, by no means, is a client State of USA. Contrarily, it is a pain in the US neck.

India must know and practice the maxim that there are no "permanent friends or foes" for reshaping its foreign policy competently. Ideological forces have disappeared from the international scene.

Pragmatism is in the ascendant. India must recognize and evaluate its national needs and interests, because national interest alone is the all-encompassing coordinate that accurately structures a country's foreign policy.

India's immediate goal in international power politics was to become an equal member of the nuclear suppliers group. That has now been achieved with the Nuclear Suppliers Group (NSG) accepting India as a responsible nuclear power, of course, with help of USA. As a reciprocal gesture, it is absolutely in our national interest to oppose nuclear proliferation, especially within and near our regional boundaries, as it affects our security. Whether it is Pakistan or Iran, possession of nuclear weapons of mass destruction by them poses danger to us. Our opposition to Iran's nuclear stand is dictated by our own national interest. It is not surrender to USA.

India's voting for the IAEA resolution, critical of Iran, has been interpreted in some quarters as kowtowing to USA. But former foreign secretary Shyam Saran's forthright arguments favouring a new global non-proliferation order show that the vote wasn't a one-off, *ad hoc* reflex—rather, it was backed by an articulated and coherent sense of India's foreign policy priorities.

India's proclivities are independent of both US and Iran. They put Indian interests first. India has objected to American double standards in upbraiding Iran, but indulging Pakistan whose nuclear advisor A.Q. Khan set up a nuclear Wal-Mart.

It must be noted here that western countries and major world powers, too, cannot escape the charge of proliferation. China has been extending nuclear know-how to North Korea and Pakistan. Israel's nuclear capabilities have been gained with West's connivance. Pakistan's nuclear scientists have smuggled sensitive data from western countries. Moreover, India cannot be expected to fight for other countries' interests at the cost of its own interests. Therefore, India has to continue to oppose Iran in IAEA voting, irrespective the hue and cry by the Left parties.

The foregoing observations on Indian Foreign Policy provide a perspective for understating India's relations with major world powers, immediate region, a large number of other countries and the UN.

India's greatest foreign policy frustration has been its unwholesome relations with its immediate neighbours. The major SAARC countries are culturally so close but politically so averse to neighbourly feelings with India. A ramification of the US presence in Afghanistan and Iraq is its closer watch on Bangladesh, Nepal and Pakistan. All these countries have terrorists of various hues operating against India, with the State connivance and even State backing. Major western powers that were callously indifferent, after 9/11 Terrorist Attack on USA have become alive to the terrorist threat emanating from these countries. These countries are infested with Osama or Maoist (link between the two is more than suspected) elements and bases. The entire western world is in a state of scare of the terrorist threat, especially the Islamic terrorism. They also know that Pakistan and Bangladesh are harbouring dangerous terrorists. Uncle Sam's overseeing these countries is a minor relief to India, as it is no longer alone while countering the nefarious terrorist designs.

India has been tolerant and accommodative toward its immediate neighbours, keeping them in productive engagement.

Relations with ASEAN and Singapore are the cornerstones of our "Look East" policy. "India-ASEAN Partnership for Peace, Progress, and Shared Prosperity" lays out a short to medium term road map of India-ASEAN cooperation in various sectors, such as economic, science and technology, information and communication technology, agriculture, health, pharmaceuticals and people to people contacts. India-ASEAN Free Trade Agreements are a continuing process.

Russia remains India's biggest supplier of defence equipment and has given assurance on the supply of spares and made new offers on equipment. India, too, is supporting Russia in its accession to the WTO and its being treated as a market economy in anti dumping investigations.

Lastly, we must remember that "in the world beyond parliaments, the press and think tanks, ideologies are being jettisoned to survive. Only the fittest will act internationally and manage change". Will India change and choose a foreign policy befitting the challenge of times? Nation States are interdependent and foreign policy is now a central part of a nation's political programme. War and Terrorism are everybody's nightmare.

"May the pens of the diplomats not ruin again what the people have attained with such exertions." Lord Palmerston's this 19th century wish is today the 21st century India's fear!

■■■

The Telangana Issue

Telangana issue has been generating a lot of news for the past couple of years. It's an issue about which many people have been very passionate and has led to the loss of many lives. Infact the Telangana issue has been around for over many years now. Here is a look at what has happened over the years and why the Telangana issue still stands unsolved as it does today.

What is Telagana?

Telangana is a region in Andhra Pradesh and was originally a princely state, ruled by the erstwhile Nizam of Hyderabad. Andhra Pradesh today as it stands, can be divided into three regions – Telangana, Rayalaseema and Coastal Andhra.

The Telangana region comprises of districts in Western and Central Andhra Pradesh (Adilabad, Karimnagar, Nizamabad, Medak, Warangal, Khammam, Hyderabad, Rangareddy, Nalgonda, and Mahaboobnagar) It comprises 10 of Andhra Pradesh's 23 districts. It accounts for 119 seats out of the 294 seats in Assembly.

Telegana at the time of Independence

After Independence, the Nizam of Hyderabad wanted to retain his hold over the state. But the Government of India had other plans and amalgamated his state on 17th September 1948 by force. On a historic note, Rayalseema and Coastal Andhra were part of the Madras Province under the British Empire. However post independence Rayalaseema and Coastal Andhra were separated from the Madras State in 1953 and were merged with the

Telangana region of Hyderabad in 1956 to form the state of Andhra Pradesh. The remaining parts of the Telangana region were merged with Karnataka and Maharashtra. This was the first state that was carved out on linguistic lines in the country.

Demands for a Separate Telangana State

Demands for carving out a separate Telangana State became more buoyant during 1969. There are quite a few reasons for this:

- There were distinct differences between Telangana and Andhra Regions.
- Andhra that was initially a part of Madras presidency had much better standards of development and education. Telangana on the other hand was more feudal in its approach and much less developed.
- The Telangana people had reservations also because they feared they would lose out on many jobs with the merger.
- The cultural differences too were apparent. Under the rule of the Nizam the Telangana region bore influences of Northern India. The kind of festivals being celebrated too was different.

The 1969 Agitation

This was primarily a student protest which erupted in the regions of Telangana with Osmania Univeristy proving to be the hot bed of it all. The protests became massive with huge numbers of people taking part in the agitation. Over 350 people lost their lives in lathi charge and police firing. Former Congress leader Channa Reddy who defected to form his own party the 'Telangana Praja Samithi' later diluted the impact of the agitation as he merged with the Congress. Channa Reddy was also the same person responsible for raising slogans like 'Jai Telangana'. The Prime Minister Indira Gandhi later went on to make him the Chief Minister after which the movement collapsed. After this P.V Narasimha Rao was also made the Chief Minister in 1971. He was also from the Telangana region.

The Role of K Chandrasekhar Rao

K Chandrasekhar Rao was a member of the Telugu Desam Party (TDP) during the 1990's. While hoping for a ministerial birth he only got that of a deputy speaker following the 1999 elections. KCR quit TDP in 2001 and set about to form the Telangana Rashtra Samithi (TRS) which he announced would fight for the formation of a separate Telangana State. The timing could not have been more perfect for KCR considering the fact the people of Telangana were already feeling looted. There was already a strong feeling gaining ground that the surplus produced by them was being rerouted to the finance body so that it could be used to develop the rest of the state.

In the elections of 2004 YS Rajashekara Reddy and KCR decided to join hands after YSR promised him the formation of a separate Telangana State. But later YSR backtracked and sent a report to the Congress against the formation of the Telangana State. TRS withdrew support from the Congress led coalition government on the grounds of alleged indecision by the government over the delivery of its electoral promise to create a separate Telangana state.

Soon the Telangana also ended up being a deeply political issue. Parties could often be seen flip flopping on their stand on the Telangana issue. The Congress and TDP are a divided house while Praja Rajyam and CPM are for a united Andhra. On the other hand the BJP and CPi are supporting the formation of s separate Telangana.

On November 29, 2009, KCR took a fast until death demanding that the Congress Government introduce the Telangana bill in the parliament. Student's rallies and people from various organizations took part in the demands and there were massive protests in many regions of Telangana. With KCR's health fast failing the centre was forced to look into issue and finally gave into his request of a separate state making KCR end his 11 day fast.

Srikrishna committee headed by Justice BN Srikrishna was then set-up to look into wether a separate state should be carved out or a united Andhra must remain. The committee was constituted by the Government of India in 3 February 2010 and expected to submit its report on 30 December 2010 to the Ministry of Home Affairs. As part of the committee they invited people from all sections of the society and also toured the entire state where they got the opinions of a lot of people on what they felt about the issue. The Sri Krishna Report was released on the internet to the public on 6 January 2011. The issue is still being contemplated in the political circles.

■ ■ ■

Women Empowerment

When it comes to women there have been a few important happenings in the recent past. For the Indian women there were the 73rd and 74th Amendments (1993) to the Constitution, providing for the reservation of seats in the local bodies of panchayats and municipalities and, of course, the post 1995 measures by the government that formed the icing. It is a different issue that the cake was missing.

The government of India had floated zealously its grand ideas for the country by declaring the year 2001 as Women's Empowerment Year, with a focus on achieving the "vision in the new century of a nation where women are equal partners with men".

What followed was a spate of programmes and schemes with fine names: *Swashakti* and *Stree Shakti* for women's empowerment; *Swayam Siddha* to benefit nearly a lakh women through micro-credit programmes, *Balika Samrudhi Yojana* for the girl child and a horde of various other projects, doubtlessly with intentions of going about a greater common good.

Today, 125 million primary school age children are not in school; most of them are girls. The current literacy rate for women in India stands at 54.16 per cent, *vis-a-vis* that of 75 per cent for males.

Efforts are, however, on for raising the standard of the girl child. There are several programmes being undertaken.

Economic Status

Women are the major contributors in terms of economic output, but their contribution still remains to be made visible. Men and women are not equally distributed across the types of work. Women are concentrated in the primary sector and in unskilled and marginal work. 95 per cent of women, as against 89 per cent men, are engaged in unorganised sector, and most of them are found in the rural areas. According to the 2001 census, 90 million women constitute the workforce.

Industries that employ more women than men include, processing of edible nuts, domestic services, bidi manufacturing, spinning, weaving, finishing of coir textiles etc. Women also constitute majority of the workforce employed as nurses, ayahs, paramedics and technical workers. Their contribution goes unnoticed as most of the times they are involved as unpaid or home-based workers, who often get counted as non-working housewives.

In last one decade the Union and State governments have envisaged the eradication of poverty through women-oriented programmes, as a major chunk of the population below the poverty line remains the hapless women. The women can also be benefited in a large measure through generating adequate amount of legal awareness and helping them in making efforts to farm collectively, as is being done by the Deccan Development Society (DDS) in Andhra Pradesh.

Marriage and Reproductive Health

Although the practice of child marriage is history for most, it still continues to be a reality of life in the rural India, especially in the North and West pockets of the country. Every once in a while, there are shocking incidents (which make it to the covers of popular magazines and hit the front pages of newspapers because of the element of horrific unusualness). The news stirs up people, only to fade away in a couple of days when the oddity has turned boring.

Child marriages, banned by law, continue to take place and yet there is no action against this practice. No amount of legislation will be effective as long as the political will to promote gender equity is absent.

The Dowry Prohibition Act has been in force for five decades, and yet, countless atrocities are perpetrated as a result of this despicable practice that finds favour with scores of the households. Marrying off a boy not only marks an easy road to prosperity, but also is seen as redemption of money spent on the daughter's wedding.

Girls in early teens are "traded off" in the name of marriage to men who are older by nothing less than twenty to twenty five years, for a certain amount of money. This saves them the hassle of dowry as well as the search for a groom! The common practice in rural India is to marry the girls around the age of fourteen or fifteen, triggering off an early motherhood for most. Quite the reason for the reproductive health scenario not being so encouraging.

Another complexity that leaves the women at cross roads is fear of the apparent persecution if she bears a daughter. The startling fact is that, on the whole, women themselves prefer a male child despite the negative impact of this mindset on their lives. This seems to be a culturally conditioned choice. This is also the reason why technologies like ultrasound and amniocentesis are being used to determine sex of the child in the womb. The apathy towards the gender inequities is evident in the classes that are expected to deliver better.

Domestic Violence

The phenomenon of domestic violence is widely prevalent, but has remained largely unseen. Millions of Indian women have, by and large, grown to accept spousal violence and, worse still, being subjected to humiliation and indignity which cripple them mentally. Afraid of the law, men may not commit acts of violence, but, in turn, resort to psychologically pressurising the woman, which has results still worse in nature.

According to the Crime Records Bureau of the Union Home Ministry, of all cases of crime committed against women every year, almost 37 per cent are cases of domestic violence. Then, there are women—especially those belonging to the middle and upper middle classes—who keep quiet for the sake of the family's image. There's more to domestic violence than physical abuse. Emotional trauma can be far more crippling.

Legislative Status

Women in India have made major inroads in various male-dominated professions, including the governmental bureaucracy. In the fields of business, medicine, engineering, law, art and culture, women who were given opportunities to acquire the necessary skills and education have proven themselves capable of holding their own, without availing of any special measures to facilitate their entry. But they have failed to gain ground in the field of politics. Moreover, the agenda of women's empowerment seems to have lost the kind of moral and political legitimacy it enjoyed during the freedom movement, as was evident from the ugly scenes in the aftermath of tabling of the Women's Reservation Bill in the Parliament.

The very same male party leaders who compete with each other in announcing their support of special reservations for women, have shown little willingness to include women in party decision-making, or even to help create a conducive atmosphere for women's participation in their own organizations.

In fact, women's marginalisation is even more pronounced in the day-to-day functioning of almost all political parties, than in the Parliament. Therefore, it is urgently required that we take special measures to enhance women's political participation. Our democracy will remain seriously flawed if it fails to yield adequate space to women.

■ ■ ■

Does TV Reflect Reality?

Medium of television continues to be under scanner. Questions that still have not got clear-cut answers are: whether television as a media reflects reality or create it? Should media portray an ideal world? What is the overall impact of the media upon reality? What should the role of the media be? Can TV actually change reality?

The best answer seems to be that the relationship is reciprocal; the media, especially TV, sometimes changes culture, while cultural changes are reflected (and legitimated) in the media.

Meida that purports to reflect 'reality'—TV news channels—has two functions. The first is to reflect reality in roughly the same proportion as is present in the real world. And the second is to develop a consensus on how that reality can be improved.

But the responsibility is more serious upon those that are, ostensibly, mainstream 'reality' media. And in India, they fail completely. For one, they focus on only one slice of reality—celebrity, for instance—with such an overwhelming passion, that they neglect to realise that the impact of this slice of reality is negligible in the larger perspective of the real world.

Such media does reflect slices of unavoidable reality sometimes—earthquakes, famines, droughts—but this coverage is so sanitised, so devoid of context, that far from becoming a stimulus for thought and action, it becomes a convenient salve to numb our sense of responsibility.

Today, television news also displays "too much reality" which, as T.S. Eliot said, humankind cannot stand. In addition, instead of shocking people into action, a daily procession and constant repetition of blood, gore and body bags has the opposite effect of familiarity reducing intensity, breeding apathy and insensitivity.

Whenever tragedy hits our country and our TV crewmen get there in time, there is a tendency to capture dead and mutilated bodies on camera and then beam them across the world. This was never truer than in the case of the television coverage of the 26/11 terror strikes in Mumbai.

What is unfortunate is when, by sinister commercial design or apathy, one kind of information is foisted upon an audience such that they slowly forget that there is an alternative. News nowadays on TV tilts toward entertainment and entertainers.

Media houses, through this brand of 'celebrity' journalism, appear to be effectively serving a group of people whose concerns revolve around fashion, glamour and celebrity. So who is responsible for the triumph of "infotainment" over information? It is us, the consumers of the news.

We allow television to be our main source of news, and this leads to critical distortions in our lives. Different perspectives, analysis and comment in features in the print media, and discussions and analyses on TV are very necessary today for the average watcher/reader to make sense of what is happening around him/her. Too much information is overwhelming and is passively received (or missed entirely) without absorption or involvement.

Family's Distorted Reality

Media that is clearly for entertainment does not need to necessarily reflect reality at all times. However, these ought to enrich us, make us feel more, think harder, challenge our assumptions, hold us in thrall by the sheer quality. One cannot find any serial which does that or the one which mirrors reality.

Although most serials do not represent reality, they seem like reality, and they produce real emotions, and tangible emotional responses, such as laughing and crying, in the audience. This creates a powerful illusion of reality, which becomes part of the emotional experience of each audience member. This emotional legacy becomes, in a sense, indistinguishable from the legacy of real life experiences. In other words, serials do not merely reflect reality, they change reality by interacting with the minds of the viewers.

In private channels, undeveloped, rural India has disappeared and in its place we often have a transformed ethnicised 'countryside' where the only structures are havelis set against a desert backdrop as seen in advertisements. The office is a far less popular setting, as are schools and colleges in serials. The concurrent professional and livelihood struggles are not given due display on the tube.

Marriage remains the anchor for the assertion of the family, so much so that individual rights are subsumed to the collective welfare of the family.

What is surprising, however, is that even the fairly huge channel-watching middle class is not represented in the serials currently dominating the media; it is as if this class does not relate to its own social experience, so ubiquitous is the world of the rich.

Earlier, the serials dealt with social issues and the assertion of women like *Rajni* or serials like *Buniyaad* and *Hum Log*—far more realistic depictions of lower and middle class values—and on subjects revolving around the underprivileged in *Nukkad* (which was set on a street corner in Mumbai). But, with the entry of private channels in the early 1990s, television programmes began to demonstrate more commitment to attracting advertisers than to social issues.

Very occasionally a serial breaks the norm, but here also the other woman is portrayed as unbalanced, slightly on the edge, and completely without morals.

When these soap operas do mirror society, it is through its ugly face, though sex determination test being carried out on a foetus, by showing a blind, helpless woman being raped by a family member and a woman committing sati. It can be said that it is wrong to blame television for all the wrongdoings in society. These things did exist in the society before. But then, what about the social responsibility of serial makers?

Fiction Wipes out Non-fiction

Certain formats have become a rarity on the Indian screen—children's serials or entertainment cum instructive ones like The Discovery of India. Period pieces, like Mirza Ghalib, too, are seldom seen. Chat shows invariably deal with persona who are rich and famous and obviously cater to a vicarious pleasure derived from getting an inside view at the personal lives of the 'beautiful' people featured on it

Shows like KBC, which promise big money, big sets and big stars can and do enforce among lads norms of getting 'easy money' without any hard work.

There is no place for the documentaries that attempted to conscientise the middle classes on various themes.

The Sleaze Game

Ideally TV should present a dimension that films cannot. Instead they mimic. This is borne out by the plethora of film-based programming, screening of films both old and new, as also like film awards live shows on TV.

Explicit sex of the most crude and vulgar kind, in the guise of song and dance sequences, with horrible pelvic thrusts, heaves of the bosom and bottom wiggling of the most vulgar sort, unabashed bedroom scenes, mindless story lines and gory violent scenes are the hallmark of film-based programming. They make one wonder what effect this kind of porn in Indian contexts can have on impressionable young Indian minds.

Also, most of the American serials are so steeped in local American contexts and values that surely they are more a form of escape for Yuppie viewers, who feel perhaps modern and international when watching them. Moreover, showing successful characters with superficial problems, such as those on Seinfeld or Friends, may give youth unrealistic expectations. Lastly, while it is necessary for Indian TV to be exposed to culture of all lands, including America, the trick is not "to be blown off feet by any of them".

Is Reality TV 'real'?

Finally, we discuss the new fad, reality programmes on TV. Reality television has the power to attract attention by alluding the viewers to think that they are seeing real people and real events. However, reality television is not what its name suggests. Besides unlashing an element of voyeurism in the audience, the characters that are portrayed by reality television are not real people. They are, in fact, the creation of producers, editors and camera crews. The social context that is presented and the story line that accompanies it are constructed for the viewer, based on what may have once been reality.

Audiences negotiate meaning in media. Even though media carries messages, they aren't received by everybody the same way. How we respond to a film, a song, or TV series is coloured by our own personal package of attitudes, values and experience. But some meanings end up being more widely accepted than others, a fact that reflects the relative clout, or social power, of the filters which affect our different readings.

Media productions are not "windows on reality", whatever their producers might like us to believe. They're deliberate constructions, the result of a series of choices.

Thus, if television is holding a mirror up to real life, it is a fun-house mirror.

■ ■ ■

Social Structure in India

The ethnic and linguistic diversity of India is proverbial and rivals the diversity of continental Europe which is not a single nation-State like India. India contains a large number of different regional, social, and economic groups, each with distinctive or dissimilar customs and cultural practices.

Region-wise, differences between social structures of India's north and south are marked, especially with respect to kinship systems and family relationships. Religious differences are pervasive through out the country.

There is the Hindu majority and the large Muslim minority or "second majority". There are other Indian groups—Buddhists, Christians, Jains, Jews, Parsis, Sikhs, and practitioners of tribal religions—and hundreds of sub-religions or religious communities within larger communities like the Arya Samajis, Sanatanis among the Hindus; Shias and Sunnis among the Muslims; Monas and Keshdharis among Sikhs and hundreds of other castes, sub-castes, communities, vegetarians and non-vegetarians from each religion. Each group is proud of its faith and very sure of its superiority over other faiths.

A highly noticeable feature of India's social structure is highly inequitable division of the nation's wealth. Access to wealth and power varies sharply.

Extreme differences in socio-economic status are glaringly visible among the smallest village communities to metropolitan cities and mega-towns.

Social Structure in India

The poor and the rich live side by side in urban and rural areas. Prosperous, well-fed, perfumed men or women in chauffeured luxury cars passing and even living in narrow streets with poor, starving, ill-nourished, ill-clad or even half-naked men, women, children dwelling on their pavements and bathing in dirty water of its flowing or even clogged drains are common sights.

Contrasting extreme poverty and enormous wealth and obvious class distinctions are egregiously visible in almost every settlement in India.

Urban-rural differences too are immense. Over 70 per cent of India's population lives in villages; agriculture still remains their mainstay. Mud houses, dusty lanes, grazing cattle, chirping and crying of birds at sunset and rising smell of dung and chulah-smoke are the usual settings for the social lives of most rural Indians.

In India's enlarging cities, millions of people live among roaring vehicles, surging crowds, overcrowded streets, busy commercial establishments, loudspeakers blaring movie tunes or religious recitations, factories and trucks and buses breathing poisonous pollution into unhealthy lungs.

Gender distinctions are highly pronounced. The behaviour norms of men and women are very different, more so in villages.

Prescribed ideal gender roles are fast losing to new patterns of behaviour among both sexes. Individually, both men and women behave in one way and collectively in quite another way.

Public behaviour of both men and women is rude and unhelpful, but the same people when in individual situation and relationship can be very different. People occupying public positions are extremely unhelpful and even normal actions done toward others as part of normal routine are projected as personal favours. Even senior citizens, retired persons, war widows do not get their pension approved for years! A clerk in a government office wields greater actual power than a decision-making executive and can withhold implementation of his superior's orders for ever.

If the victim of delay approaches the court, the litigant is in for a shock after shock as the case gets adjourned endlessly and after years of attending court hearings gets an unimaginably skewed judgement written in a highly ambiguous language. Litigants pay high fees to lawyers and bribes to court staff and even to judges.

Surprisingly, observers tend to bypass these all-pervading differences of region, language, wealth, status, religion, urbanity, gender and absence of the rule of law but pay most devoted attention to that special and peculiar feature of Indian society: "CASTE". The most loved and recognized identity of Indians is their caste.

And, there are thousands of castes and caste-like groups. These are hierarchically ordered and named groups into which members are born. Caste members, as far as possible, marry within the caste or sub-caste and follow caste rules with respect to diet, ritual and aspects of life.

Yet, no generalization can be made because, increasingly, caste- discipline is loosening and every individual is free to decide her or his own social ways and such an indivi-dual will always find small or big support and a milieu to evolve a suitable mode of living in spite of turning her/his back on caste and caste-ridden society, though at times, this can be a harrowing experience, especially in sub-caste communities where inter-caste and widow marriage is equated with community honour leading to honour-killing of the perceived violator of caste-norms, especially if the violator is weak.

However, underlying norms of life, though honesty of thought and action may not be among them, are widely accepted in India.

Indian city dwellers are often nostalgic about "simple village life", but Indian villages have been losing both simplicity and gaiety of life and are boiling in the caste cauldron of petty rivalries. They are afflicted with addiction to all kinds of drugs like alcohol, opium and heroin. Roads, television and mobile phones are now changing the village scene though dirt, squalor and disease still vitiate rural India.

Indian village life is neither simple nor inviting. That is why no villager who has come to the city goes back. According to sociologists: "Each village is connected through a variety of crucial horizontal linkages with other villages and with urban areas both near and far.

Most villages are characterized by a multiplicity of economic, caste, kinship, occupational, and even religious groups linked vertically within each settlement. Factionalism is a typical feature of village politics.

In one of the first of the modern anthropological studies of Indian village life, anthropologist Oscar Lewis called this complexity "rural cosmopolitanism."

Typical Indian villages have clustered dwelling patterns built very close to one another. Sociologists call them "nucleated settlements", with small and narrow lanes for passage of people and sometimes carts. Village fields surround these settlements. On the hills of central, eastern, and far northern India, dwellings are more spread out. In wet States of West Bengal and Kerala, houses are a little dispersed; in Kerala, some villages merge into the next village and visitor are not able to see divisions between such villages.

In northern and central India, neighbourhood boundaries can be vague. Houses of Dalits are ordinarily situated on outskirts of nucleated settlements. Distinct Dalit hamlets, however, are rare.

Contrastingly, in the south, where socio-economic divisions and caste pollution observances tend to be stronger than in the north, Dalit hamlets are set at a little distance from other caste neighbourhoods.

Bigger landowners do not cultivate lands but hire tenant farmers to do this work. Artisans in pottery, wood, cloth, metal, and leather, although diminishing, continue to eke out their existence in contemporary Indian villages like centuries past. Religious observances and weddings are occasions for members of various castes to provide customary ritual goods and services.

Accelerating urbanization is fast transforming Indian society. More than 26 per cent of the country's population is urban. India's larger cities have been growing at twice the rate of smaller towns and villages.

About half of the increase is the result of rural-urban migration, as villagers seek better lives for themselves in the cities.

Most Indian cities are densely populated. New Delhi, for example, had 6,352 people per square kilometre in

1991. Congestion, noise, traffic jams, air pollution, grossly inadequate housing, transportation, sewerage, electric power, water supplies, schools, hospitals and major shortages of key necessities characterize urban life.

Slums and pavement dwellers constantly multiply so also trucks, buses, cars, auto-rickshaws, motorcycles, and scooters, spewing uncontrolled fumes, all surging in haphazard patterns along with jaywalking pedestrians and cattle.

A recent phenomenon is illegal migrants from neighbouring Bangladesh and terrorists via Nepal, Bangladesh and Pakistan. They stalk all big cities and State capitals and strike at will. India's city life is extremely insecure and crime-infested.

Once a sleepy land of docile people, India has become one of the 20 most dangerous countries of the world to live in.

■ ■ ■

NSG Waiver and Indo-US Nuclear Deal

Was it an Indian achievement? Has it catapulted India into the P-5 league? Will India become powerful and prosperous now? Will India be empowered to eradicate its chronic poverty after the NSG waiver and the Nuclear Deal with the USA? These issues need to be discussed dispassionately because these potentially epoch-making events are enveloped in a good deal of ambiguity and confusion in spite of prolonged debate and negotiations.

"For the first time", says a senior official, "we have brought the international system to a point where it suits us. India has entered the nuclear mainstream."

The government has reasons to be effusive because, for the first time, India found the USA backing it to the hilt and President Bush personally cajoled all the lesser and smaller states like Austria, New Zealand, Ireland and Switzerland to make it a unani-mous vote for a very special consideration shown to India.

Internationally, for all intents and purposes, it was a United State's initiative, and not an Indian achievement. Is it also obvious, then, that the waiver achieves the US objective more than the Indian goals?

Domestically, the Indo-US deal kicked up a good deal of political dust and the usually modest, academic Prime Minister Manmohan Singh changed colours, emerging as a wheeling-dealing politician who used all kinds of tactics and temptations to win a vote of confidence on the Nuclear Deal issue, abandoning his Communist-led Left allies and embracing Mulayam-Amar Singh-led Samajwadi Party, till then a sworn enemy of Manmohan-Sonia-led Congress, the leading constituent of the UPA government. According to a journalist, "he has earned his place in history as the leader who wears two crowns—unshackling India at home through economic reforms and liberating it abroad from nuclear apartheid", though he has lost the high moral ground that he occupied in these times of plummeting standards of public life.

No doubt, the NSG waiver and Indo-US civil nuclear agreement have brought India and the USA closer than ever and India is now on the thresh-hold of a new foreign policy paradigm.

The era of Nehru and Indira Gandhi when India pursued an independent foreign policy in times of great risks, as in 1971 Bangladesh war or UK-France-Israel attack on Egypt, is about to end.

Yet, a deal is as good as one makes it. If Indian politicians and diplomats show grit and national commitment, the USA, a weakening superpower, facing economic confusion and overstretched in its militarist engagement in Asia, can also be made to bend favourably to Indian interests.

Currently, however, the US interest in India is more political than commercial because the USA is not in the forefront of nuclear reactor technology and is not building nuclear power stations domestically, while India's priority is to go on a buying spree and make good its energy deficit.

The above point, however, was underscored by the attitude of Democrat-dominated US Senate. The Senate was inclined to "get this done" only after "modifications". New Delhi's announcements about self-imposed moratorium on nuclear tests appeared to have had no impact on the US Senate. Senators, unwilling to wave aside the charges of non-proliferation hardliners, continued to remain stringent and skeptic about India's being a non-signatory to NPT.

President Bush kept trying to convince the Senate on the questions of fuel guarantees written into the deal as merely a political commitment, though India believes them legally binding under international law.

Who was correct? Bush's chief negotiator, William Burns, beat about the bush [no pun intended] to keep Delhi calm but finally conceded that US has made no more than "political commitments" and the "Indians do understand that our actions will be guided by US law".

Burns said Congress should okay the deal at once since currently India had a political leadership that was agreeable to US Administration's terms and immediate passage would offer a level playing field to US businesses, which would otherwise be disadvantaged if other countries took advantage of the NSG clearance and penetrate Indian market in advance.

While India maintains a sovereign right to test, US can call off the deal should India test without mitigating reasons, appears to be the basis of the deal.

Much will depend on how soon India begins to feel and act like a great political power and increase its negotiability internationally.

The USA is clearly looking in India an ally who would demonstrate its power and capacity to stabilise Asia so that the USA is free to make its foray far afield into the sphere of Russian influence in Asia and keep a watch over overly ambitious China. The USA befriended China when both of them were anti-Russia but now China is perceived as a rival in Asia, if not in the rest of the world.

At present, India's negotiability is limited to its big business offer to the USA. "The Indian government has provided the US with a strong Letter of Intent, stating its intention to purchase reactors with at least 10,000 MW worth of new power generation capacity from US firms."

"India has committed to devoting at least two sites to US firms", said William Burns, US undersecretary for political affairs, and emphasized that "International competition will, inevitably, be intense and we want to avoid exposing US firms to any unnecessary delays".

Burns also disclosed that India would stick to the Convention on Supplementary Compensation for Nuclear Damage.

This is an internationally recognised convention and it is a prerequisite for the participation of foreign nuclear firms in India.

This is an extraordinary concession to the US Nuclear Reactor firms who have failed to get a single order to build reactors within their own country. What it means is that if a Union Carbide-like Bhopal tragedy or Chernobyl-like nuclear plant explosive disaster occurs, it will be the Indian government and not the US reactor builder who will bear liability for loss of life and property resulting from the US builder's fault or failure to take safety measures.

When terms are so easy, both Indian and foreign nuclear energy providers will make a bee-line to New Delhi in the hope of raking up the 100 billion dollar bonanza that the nuclear deal is dangling before the carpetbaggers.

Russia, as a dependable friend during the Soviet and cold war days, under Putin's leadership, is nostalgic about the old glory as superpower. Recent action in Georgia has brought Russia face to face with the USA as claimant to influence over Asia.

Economically, because of unlimited oil reserves and traditionally firm technological base and closer ties with China, Russia will not like India to become a source of strength to the USA in its initiatives in Asia.

Russia is helping Iran build nuclear station; so is China helping Pakistan build plutonium reactors and more nuclear bombs.

China is also encouraging North Korea to keep nagging USA on its nuclear deal. China is also constantly increasing its influence over Nepal, Bangladesh, Sri Lanka, Burma and its naval presence in the Indian Ocean. Australia openly prefers China to India and has refused to sell uranium to India, while it is selling it to Russia and China.

Are Indian diplomats capable of outwitting China without offending it? India's diplomatic record in its immediate and larger neighbourhood is very poor.

If Indian diplomats think that they can walk carefree holding Uncle Sam's finger, they are mistaken. The USA never lends strength free of cost and is capable of twisting arm of its allies.

India's new world environment as the sixth power is full of challenges and responsibilities: pulls from the neighbourhood, expectations on non-proliferation and Iran's nuclear quest are just three amongst many others. Domestically, India faces debilitating institutional and political strains that impede its march.

Confusion still prevails and is likely to persist even after the deal has been signed, because the question whether India will be able to purchase nuclear technology from NSG countries on its own terms will remain unanswered.

The first concrete consequence of the NSG Waiver, however, is Indo-French civil nuclear deal signed in Paris during Indian PM's visit on his way back from Washington.

■■■

Indian Democracy and Rule of Law

India is considered a well-established democracy. Looking back, it has been a momentous journey since Independence in 1947 and adoption of the Constitution on January 26, 1950. Yet, the Indian democracy has not fructified. Its constitutional goals and democratic aspirations remain unrealized.

Even though the Indian democracy has withstood six decades of social, economic, political challenges, including an 18-month long State of Emergency, the challenge to its democratic governance persists. Simply put, "The rule of law" does not prevail in India.

In fact, threats to the rule of law are relentlessly subverting Indian democracy and imperilling its system of governance in the country.

It has been proved beyond doubt that social and economic progress achieved by developed democratic societies is directly the result of their vigilant protection and enforcement of the rule of law.

The right to equality before the law, often phrased as 'equal protection of the law', is fundamental to any just and democratic society. Rich or poor, majority or minority, political ally of the State or its opponent—all are entitled to equal protection before the law.

We may argue that life does not treat every one equally and even in the same family each member has a different course of life. However, the State and its systems are the creation of man and not of fate and the State has the responsibility to treat all its citizens equally. According to the constitutional law expert John P. Frank, "Under no circumstances should the State impose additional inequalities; it should be required to deal evenly and equally with all of its people."

In a democratic State, no one is above the law. Democracy is for the people, by the people and of the people, said Abraham Lincoln. The laws in a democratic State are created in the name of the people by the elected representatives of the people. They are not supposed to be imposed upon them.

There is a sound presumption that citizens of a democracy submit to their laws because they know that they are submitting to themselves, however indirectly, as makers of laws. Once the laws have been made and the people obey them, both law and democracy prevail.

The history of every society shows that the power-holders tend to get corrupt and tyrannical. In a democracy, those who administer the criminal justice system hold great power and the potential for its abuse is inevitably there.

The State power is exercised to imprison, seize property, torture, exile and execute individuals without legal justification—and even without any formal charges being brought. A democratic society that tolerates such abuses faces the peril of curtailing its democracy and even losing it.

No State can exist without having the power to maintain order and punish criminal acts. Democratic States too must have the power to punish the wrong-doers but the rules and procedures by which the State enforces its laws must be explicit, transparent and open to the public view. Yet, no democratic State is free from secret, arbitrary and manipulative power and political trickery.

There are essential requirements of due process of law in a democracy that may be briefly described as follows:

1. No one's home can be broken into and searched by the police without a court order showing that there is good cause for such a search. The midnight knock of the secret police is repugnant to democracy.

2. No person can be arrested without manifest, written charges that specify the alleged violation. The accused are entitled to know the exact nature of the charge against them and must be released at once under the doctrine known as habeas corpus, if the court finds the charge and arrest invalid.

3. Persons charged with offence should not be held for protracted periods in prison. They must have the right to a speedy public trial, and to cross-examine their accusers.

4. The authorities must grant bail, or conditional release, to the accused pending trial, if there is little likelihood of the suspect to flee or commit other crimes. "Cruel and unusual" punishment, as determined by the traditions and laws of the society, such as community panchayat's punishing members of their community for violation of their customs, must be prohibited.

5. Persons must not be compelled to be witnesses against themselves. This prohibition must be absolute and the police must not use torture or physical or psychological abuse against suspects. A legal system that bans forced confessions stops the police from using torture, threats,

or other forms of abuse to obtain information because the court will not allow such information as evidence during trial.

6 No person shall be subject to double jeopardy; that is, no one be charged with the same offence twice.

7 The so-called *ex post facto* laws are also proscribed. These are laws made after the fact so that someone can be charged with an offence even though the act was not illegal at the time it was committed.

8 Defendants should have access to additional protections against coercive acts by the State. For example, in the United States the accused have a right to a lawyer who represents them at all stages of a criminal proceeding, even if the accused is not able to pay for such legal service.

The police must inform suspects of their rights at the time of their arrest, including the right to have a lawyer and the right to remain silent for avoiding being witness against themselves.

Though efforts have been made to enforce and institutionalise the rule of law in India they have not achieved the intended results. We cannot say that the normative framework of constitutional governance does not exist in the country. This has been provided by India's Constitution and many institutions have also been established under it. However, no deep values have been ingrained, nor unassailable principles, as directed by the Constitution, are being practiced by India's institutions. As a result, the Indian society is bereft of the benefits of constitutionalism.

Six decades of governance should have been long

enough for a country like India with a very long tradition of Satyamev Jayate to develop institutions whose working would reflect both inherited and acquired values of enlightenment and rational social and political conduct.

All that our institutions have done is to rouse high social expectations with a modicum of their fulfilment. The abuse of power has, in fact, become a universal phenomenon.

The Indian judiciary enjoys good reputation both nationally and internationally for its progressive interpretation of various provisions of the Constitution that has helped promote the cause of social justice. Judicial interpretations have expanded the scope of our fundamental rights as enshrined in the Constitution.

Higher Judiciary has also helped overcome restrictions on rules relating to locus standi and created new avenues for seeking remedies for violation of human rights. It has allowed public interest litigation petitions and genuinely intervened in the areas of child labour, bonded labour, clean and healthy environment, and women's rights, to cite a few instances of judicial intervention. Such judicial interventions on behalf of human rights have been successful in upholding the rule of law.

But, in view of the vast and unmitigated violations of justice, these judicial achievements simply pale into insignificance. The scale of prevailing inequalities and violations of human and fundamental rights have made the Indian democratic State look like a despotic dispensation.

Enforcing the rule of law itself remains a fundamental challenge, leave aside other innumerable crises of the Indian legal system. We do have the laws, but no implementation of these laws; we have a vast body of rules that are followed more in their violation than in their observation.

The behaviour of those who govern is highly reprehensible. They have no respect for the laws of the land. Citizens too have ceased to care for the laws and be law-abiding. This lack of respect for laws by the government and the people at large is becoming a most serious threat to Indian democracy. The Indian people are fast losing trust and faith in the democratic institutions.

Passing more laws and establishing more institutions is causing what appears to be an organized confusion in the legal system of the country. Plethora of laws and increasing number of Tribunals, Rights Commissions and Forums are only increasing the role and size of the insensitive bureaucracy in the system of governance.

They are creating and perpetuating an unjust society that the people now accept as a fact to live with. There is need for a fundamental re-examination of the approaches that have been adopted to enforce the rule of law and critically examine the effectiveness of Indian democracy.

A report of the National Commission to Review the Working of the Constitution in India noted: "The paradox of India, however, is that in spite of a vigilant press and public opinion, the level of corruption is exceptionally high. This may be attributed to the utter insensitivity, lack of shame and the absence of any sense of public morality among the bribe-takers. Indeed, they wear their badge of corruption and shamelessness with equal élan and brazenness."

In the last decade there has been an expansion of legal education. Innumerable law schools and universities have come up but the ethical standards in the legal profession have sunk very low. Both judges and advocates now indulge in corrupt practices. The law itself favours the criminals; complainants and witnesses suffer the most in the crowded courts and through interminable trials. Adjournments have become a bane of almost every court, highest and lowest in the whole country. Neither the judges nor the successful lawyers now inspire the youth. They have created an unbridgeable gap between the law as it obtains in the books and the law as it is actually practiced in the courts of diverse description.

Democracy and the rule of law are inextricably connected. Urgent steps are needed to establish a rule of law society in India or else our credibility as a democracy will get destroyed.

■■■

The Issue of Energy Problems

Most of us are likely to miss out on the fact that there are almost 70,000 products that require petroleum as the basic constituent. This includes plastics, acrylics, cosmetics, paints, varnishes, asphalt, fertilizers, medications, etc. To boot, we are sharing these essentials with six billion other individuals who dwell here!

The accomplishments of civilization have largely been achieved through increasingly efficient and extensive harnessing of various forms of energy. Energy is indispensable for human development and economic growth. Global primary energy use has been expanding by about 2 per cent a year.

The International Energy Agency (IEA) estimates that gas consumption would rise to approach that of coal. Hydroelectric power and renewables would rise steadily, but levels on the whole will remain low. As for nuclear power, consumption is expected to stabilise by 2020.

Renewables

Many experts believe that hydrogen, wind and solar power will provide most of the world's energy in 50 years, with fossil fuels playing a smaller role. And, conservation is important for this transition.

Solar energy can be used to meet our electricity requirements. Through Solar Photovoltaic (SPV) cells, solar radiation gets converted into DC electricity directly. This electricity can either be used as it is or can be stored in the battery. This stored electrical energy then can be used at night. SPV can be used for a number of applications such as domestic lighting, street lighting, village electrification, water pumping, desalination of salty water, powering of remote telecommunication repeater stations and railway signals.

Biomass is a renewable energy resource derived from carbonaceous waste of various human and natural activities. It is derived from numerous sources, including the by-products of timber industry, agricultural crops, raw material from the forest, major parts of household waste and wood. Hydroelectric power is currently the world's largest renewable source of electricity, accounting for 6% of worldwide energy supply or about 15% of the world's electricity.

Wind energy systems for irrigation and milling have been in use since ancient times and since the beginning of the 20th century it is being used to generate electric power. Wind turbines transform the energy in the wind into mechanical power, which can then be used directly for grinding etc. or further converting to electric power to generate electricity. Wind turbines can be used singly or in clusters called "wind farms". Small wind turbines called aero-generators can be used to charge large batteries.

Five nations—Germany, USA, Denmark, Spain and India—account for 80% of the worlds installed wind energy capacity. Wind energy continues to be the fastest growing renewable energy source with worldwide wind power installed capacity reaching 14,000 MW. India ranks 5th in the world with a total wind power capacity of more than 1080 MW. In India, States of Tamil Nadu and Gujarat lead in the field of wind energy.

Tidal Energy

Energy is also obtained from waves and tides. The first wave energy project with a capacity of 150 MW, has been set up near Trivandrum. A major tidal wave power project costing of Rs. 5000 crore is proposed to be set up in the Hanthal Creek in the Gulf of Kutch in Gujarat.

Electric power plants driven by geothermal energy provide over 44 billion kilowatt hours of electricity worldwide per year, and world capacity is growing at approximately 9% per year. To produce electric power from geothermal resources, underground reservoirs of steam or hot water are tapped by wells and the steam rotates turbines that generate electricity. Typically, water is then returned to the ground to recharge the reservoir and complete the renewable energy cycle.

Underground reservoirs are also tapped for "direct-use" applications. In these instances, hot water is channelled to greenhouses, spas, fish farms, and homes to fill space heating and hot water needs.

Geothermal energy use extends beyond underground reservoirs. The soil and near-surface rocks, from 5 to 50 feet deep, have a nearly constant temperature from geothermal heating.

The Indian Scenario

India accounted for 12.5% of total primary energy consumption in the Asia-Pacific region and 3% of world's primary energy consumption. However, per capita energy consumption remains low at 486 KGOE (Kilograms of Oil Equivalent), compared with a world average of 1659 KGOE. Increasing oil and coal imports in recent years is an area of concern for the Indian energy sector.

Oil accounts for about 30% of India's total energy consumption. The majority of India's roughly 4.8 billion barrels in oil reserves are located in the Bombay High, Upper Assam, Cambay, Krisha-Godavari, and Cauvery basins.

Oil consumption in India has soared from 1.9 million bbl/d in 2001, to more than 3.4 million bbl/d by 2010. In its attempt to limit its dependence on oil imports, India is trying to expand domestic exploration and production. It is also pursuing the New Exploration Licensing Policy (NELP), announced in 1997, which permits foreign involvement in exploration, an activity long restricted to Indian State-owned firms.

Indian consumption of natural gas has risen faster than any other fuel in recent years. Natural gas use was nearly 0.8 Tcf in 1999 and has reached more than 1.8 Tcf in 2010. Increased use of natural gas in power generation is to account for most of the increase, as the Indian Government has been encouraging the construction of gas-fired electric power plants in coastal areas where they can be easily supplied with Liquefied Natural Gas (LNG) by sea.

It is most likely that the natural gas demand will out pace the supply leading to imports either via pipeline or LNG tanker.

Coal dominates the energy mix in India, contributing 70% of the total primary energy production. Power generation accounts for about 70% of India's coal consumption, followed by heavy industry. Coal consumption has increased to 427 million short tons (Mmst) in 2010, up from 348 million in 1999. India is the world's third largest coal producer (after the China and the United States), and domestic supplies satisfy most of the country's coal demand. The snag lies in the fact that Indian coal generally has a high ash content and low calorific value, so most coking coal is imported. Major fields are found in Bihar, West Bengal, and Madhya Pradesh.

Nearly all of India's 390 mines are under Coal India Ltd. (CIL), which accounts for about 90% of the country's coal production. Current policy allows private mines only if they are "captive" operations, which feed a power plant or factory. The current government has called off plans for further coal-sector liberalization in the face of strong opposition from labour unions.

Despite 80% of the population having access to electricity, the unreliability of the supplies is so severe that it impinges on the overall productivity and development of the country.

The drive to increase the country's generating capacity, along with the general trend toward economic liberalization in India in the 1990s, led to much interest among foreign inves-tors in setting up Independent Power Producers (IPPs) in India.

The government encourages the construction of mega-projects, defined as plants with capacity of more than 1,000 MW for thermal plants and more than 500 MW for hydroelectric plants, but approvals have not usually led to construction. Out of the many projects approved, several have been cancelled and a couple of them have been hanging fire.

■■■

Life Saving Drugs- Antibiotics

Antibiotics are playing an important role in our society. Sir Alexander Fleming's was a founder of antibiotics through his careful observations of 1928. Without it, many lives would have been in danger due to so many infectious diseases. Antibiotics are chemical substances produced by various species of micro-organisms and other living systems that are capable of inhibiting the growth of killing bacteria and other micro-organisms, in small concentrations.

These organisms can be bacteria, viruses, fungi or animals called protozoa. A particular group of these agents is made up of drugs called antibiotics.

Antibiotics can be bacteriostatic (bacteria stopped from multiplying) or bactericidal (bacteria killed). It is believed that antibiotics interfere with the surface of bacteria cells, causing a change in their ability to reproduce.

Antibiotics are manufactured in two ways. One of them is natural. At one time, all antibiotics were made from living organisms. This process, known as biosynthesis, is still used in the manufacture of some antibiotics. Other type is synthetic.

All penicillin types have an identical chemical nucleus called a ring. The chemical chain that is attached to the ring is different in each type. By changing the molecules of the chain, scientists devise drugs with potentially different effects on different organisms. Some of these drugs are useful in treating infections, some are not.

Pharmaceutical manufacturers now use computer-generated images of the rings and experiment with an endless variety of possible chains. Researchers have developed antibiotics which allow taking the medicine once in 24 hours instead of every few hours. The newer antibiotics are also more effective against a wider range of infections than were earlier drugs. There are dozens of antibiotics. The following are in common use:

Penicillin: The various types of Penicillin's make up a large group of antibacterial antibiotics.

Cephalosporin: These drugs are used for combating deep infections that occur in bones and those resulting from surgery.

Aminoglycoside: These drugs are used to treat tuberculosis, bubonic plague and other infections.

Tetracycline: Tetracyclines are effective against pneumonia, typhus and other bacteria-caused illness but can harm the function of the liver and kidney.

Macrolide: Macrolides are often used in patients who appear to be sensitive to Penicillin.

Polypeptide: The class of antibiotics called Polypeptides is quite toxic (poisonous) and is used mostly on the surface of the skin .

Allergic reactions to antibiotics are usually seen as rashes on the skin, but severe anaemia, stomach disorders and deafness can occasionally result. It was once thought that allergic reactions to antibiotics were frequent and permanent.

But, recent studies suggest that many people outgrow their sensitivity or never were allergic. The large numbers of antibiotics that are now available offer a choice of treatment that can avoid allergy-causing drugs.

It is well to remember that all drugs can cause both wanted and unwanted effects on the body. It is a fact that all drugs have the potential to be both beneficial and harmful.

Another use of antibiotics is, as additives to the feed of animals. Chickens and beef cattle, can be fed with these additives for better weight gains and to speed their growth.

Current work in antibiotics is largely in the area of viruses. Although some antiviral are available, most have toxic effects so severe that they can be used only in life-threatening diseases where the negative effects are the lesser danger.

Preliminary studies, however, are reporting success in the development of safer antiviral drugs and their use should be possible within the near future.

■■■

India's Achievements after Independence

India got freedom on 15th August, 1947. Many unknown heroes risked their lives so that all of us may breathe in freedom. Achieving independence was a tremendous task. After it the building of the country began in right earnest. India is heading towards major superpower in the world. During the last sixty years India has seen many up and downs.

Typically speaking, if a person reaches 60 years of age, he is labeled as an 'Old Crippled'. One can construe the picture of a man who is bed-ridden, invalid and too old to respond to any kind of treatment. He just lay aside, cherishing its blooming youthful days or he employs his time by playing with his grandchildren, but now the things have changed.

India is a 60 years old country but still very young, highly energetic and is working enthusiastically towards its betterment. India was free from the clutches of British in 1947. We still remember those stalwarts who sacrificed their lives to free us from British cage enabling us to fly freely, independently in the air. We all know and have studied umpteen numbers of times about it in our History books. We studied what all 'Our Father of the Nation'- 'Mahatma Gandhi' did, we all are aware of the Jallianwala Bagh tragedy and etc.

What makes a country good and great? - It is the people, their power of knowledge, caliber, and perseverance. Their highly intellectual minds, Decisiveness, their open and above board dealings with others. A country is empty if there are no people. We the people form our Government, We the people rule not our lives but the whole life of our stupendous country. We the people makes or mars the present, future of our country. We the people mould, shape our country in whatever manner we want to. Like, a one person cannot contribute significantly towards the prosperity, success of the country in the same manner it is not in the hands of one person to change it.

It is the collective responsibility of all and sundry to make a gloriously bright, radiant future and to be linked together in its weal and woe. We all know that it sounds the same and hackneyed but as a matter of fact this is the only transparent and solid truth. It is we the people only who back-bite and says bitchy things about our country, thus this is the major reason why our country is lacking far behind and is deprived of numerous facilities as compared to others. We all should become at home in this fact.

As our country has attained its 60 years of Independence and the prime ministers starting from Jawaharlal Nehru to Dr. Mannohan Singh talks about the developments that they will do in the fields of agriculture, industry, infrastructure, education etc and the various measures implemented towards the economic growth of our country. That their longevity of speech should not reflect about the planned tasks but about the accomplished tasks – that will be the biggest achievement of our country. Quite bummed, that so far no one has said so.

The Visible achievements made by our Country are as follows:

Metros: Eventually, Our Government has once utilized

its funds in an appropriate manner. Metros have made our lives relatively easier as the gap of communication has been minimized. The person does not have to wait for hours for buses. This is indeed a big achievement, and various other metros projects which are coming up, our country is giving business to French Government, thus ameliorating our relations.

Technology: In terms of technology, the high emergence of mobile companies, nowadays even a scrap or a vegetable vendors possess a mobile phone. The trade of mobile phone contributes 50 % towards our economic growth. Tate has created people's car of 1 crore. They are incredibly great achievements in itself.

Economy: With RBI reducing the interest rates, Sunil Mittal acquiring Arcelor, Tate acquiring Corus, with the emergence of SEZ zones , many foreign companies intruding into India to set up their business, is in itself a great achievement , but various pros and cons attached to it.

Research: Recently Ranbaxy lost over Pfizzer over a new drug, Scientists have discovered a new planet, a star etc.

Space: India has sent a space shuttle into the space. What is the outcome of that?

Indo-USA Deal is not an achievement till yet, as the major, intense, hot dispute going between the left and the Congress for their 123 agreement has put the deal in a state of uncertainty, in a high suspense. Prime Minister has strictly said LIKE it or LUMP it. But what if the Government will dissolve and the coalition government will be formed.

Entertainment: Shilpa Shetty winning the Big Brother Show, making herself an international personality in abroad, thus making of our country proud on British grounds is a great achievement in the entertainment field.

Education Sector: In a quick recap of our 2007 budget which lays emphasis on education sector is so far in the process.

Infrastructure: No doubt the infrastructure of our country has shown immense improvement with the emergence of highways, toll bridge, Metros etc.

Achievement means the thing which we have successfully acquired, attain, obtain with our hard, honest and hearty works. As mentioned above also we all are essentially self-centred, terribly selfish human beings, we want to play because we want to make centuries, we to shine in our lives, we want to create history by making our new records, but the day we start playing as a team, not for our individual selves we are sure to win a world cup.

Students and young generation plays an important role in the process of National Development. If they are good then only the sacrifices made by our known and unknown freedom fighters will be worth while. Only then India will be happy and prosperous.

■ ■ ■

Telecommuting

Telecommuting is one of the hottest topics today. It will have major effects in the worlds of work and family life. However, its biggest effect will be in the area of individual freedom, responsibility, and time management.

Work and workplaces will alter dramatically. Offices may become smaller, as fewer desks are needed. There will be greater need for high-bandwidth connections to link the office and the home, and even homes to other homes, as other employees and supervisors also begin working at home. Hours spent commuting, traffic jams, and fights for parking should diminish, as workers make fewer journeys or work staggered hours.

Family life will also change. Workers, both husbands and wives, can arrange their work around family commitments such as taking children to school, cooking, leisure activities, etc. However, households will also have to set aside areas for work – particularly if both spouses are telecommuting.

However, although the ideas of more time at home and less time traveling are attractive, there are some drawbacks to telecommuting. People may feel unable to escape their work, and may even work longer or more unsocial hours. The quality of work may suffer because of the reduced face-to-face interaction with other employees. There may be delays if other workers are not immediately available. Telecommuters may feel isolated or unmotivated, or insecure about decisions. A major change will be in the way people think about work as a place or an institution. Instead, they will focus on the task or product. Workers may feel less loyal to a company and more inclined to change jobs or work part-time or on contract.

In conclusion, the effects are difficult to predict because they depend on the extent to which telecommuting becomes popular. However, telecommuting could be the start of a major societal shift, possibly as big as the Industrial Revolution which created our present ideas of work.

■■■

Retirement at 65?

When should people be made to retire? 55? 65? Should there be a compulsory age limit? Many old people work well into their 70s and 80s, running families, countries or corporations. Other people, however, despite being fit and highly talented, are forced to retire in their or even earlier because of company or national regulations. This essay will examine whether people should be allowed to continue working for as long as they want or whether they should be encouraged to retire at a particular stage.

There are several arguments for allowing older people to continue working as long as they are able. First of all, older employees have an immense amount of knowledge and experience which can be lost to a business or organization if they are made to retire. A second point is that older employees are often extremely loyal employees and are more willing to implement company policies than younger less committed staff.

However, a more important point is regarding the attitudes in society to old people. To force someone to resign or retire at 60 or 65 indicates that the society does not value the input of these people and that effectively their useful life is over.

Allowing older people to work indefinitely however is not always a good policy. Age alone is no guarantee of ability. Many younger employees have more experience or skills than older staff, who may have been stuck in one area or unit for most of their working lives. Having compulsory retirement allows new ideas in an organization. In addition, without age limits, however arbitrary, many people would continue to work purely because they did not have any other plans or roles. A third point of view is that older people should be rewarded by society for their life's labour by being given generous pensions and the freedom to enjoy their leisure.

With many young people unemployed or frustrated in low-level positions, there are often calls to compulsorily retire older workers. However, this can affect the older individual's freedom – and right – to work and can deprive society of valuable experience and insights. I feel that giving workers more flexibility and choice over their retirement age will benefit society and the individual.

∎∎∎

Social Networking Sites: Good or Bad?

Proud of being an online network socialite? Do you Twitter about your Facebook status while listening to music on Last.fm? Have your friends noticed that you'll only talk to them 140 characters at a time? Then you've got your finger on the pulse of online social networking — a big part of Web 2.0.

Just a few years ago, the idea of an online social network was revolutionary. While the Web has always provided a way for people to make connections with one another, social networking sites made it easier than ever to find old friends and make new ones. Today, it's rare to find someone who hasn't at least heard of Facebook, MySpace, Twitter or one of a hundred other social networks.

For novices in the world of social networking, the vast online landscape can be a little intimidating. There are so many options available and each one has its own terms of service or end user license agreement (EULA). Even Web veterans may find some of these agreements difficult to understand. There are times when it can feel like you're signing your life away just to get a profile on a Web site. You may not even know why you would want to use such a site in the first place, apart from the fact that everyone else seems to be on it.

Let's break-down the positive and negative aspects of online social networking sites. Before we go much farther, understand that there are a lot of things you should take into consideration before signing up. You should also know that the good tends to outweigh the bad, particularly if you're careful about the way you use these sites. So, let's start off with the pros of social networking sites.

Without a doubt, the best reason to join any social networking site is that it lets you make connections with other people. You can use social networking sites to stay up to speed with what your friends are doing. If the social network is popular, you may be able to track down old friends and acquaintances and renew long-forgotten friendships.

You can also use these sites to network professionally. Even if you're happy where you are in your career, you might be able to help someone else out. For instance, one friend might mention on his profile that he needs a carpenter to come to his house. You might know someone who's perfect for the job. All you have to do is send a couple of messages and you've helped two friends out at the same time!

Many social networking sites like MySpace and Facebook make it easy to organise an event and invite your friends. Some sites allow you to group friends using different criteria, including geographic location. So the next time you plan a group trip to the movies, you can send out a notice to your local friends using a social networking service.

Are you an actor, musician or writer? If so, you can use social networking sites to promote your work. Many sites allow users to create special pages for bands or theater companies. You can keep fans informed about everything from your latest single to the next time you'll perform. And social networking sites gives people the opportunity to interact with the artists they admire.

Several social networking sites also act as application platforms. You can find dozens of applications ranging from quizzes to games to restaurant review programs. On a site like Facebook or MySpace, you can challenge your friend to a game of trivia -- even if she's on the other side of the world!

Social networking may even get you out of jail! American graduate student James Karl Buck was in Egypt covering an anti-government protest rally when Egyptian police detained him. Buck sent out a single word over his Twitter feed: Arrested. People following him on Twitter knew that he was in trouble and began to contact U.S. authorities. Before long, Egyptian officials had released Buck.

But it's not all sunshine and roses. There are some drawbacks to social networking too. Perhaps the biggest online social networking drawback is that it makes identity theft easier. In order to create a profile on a social networking site, you have to share some information about yourself. Many sites allow you to decide how much information to share. Some give you options to hide information like your e-mail address or birthday — information that could give unscrupulous people the chance to send you spam or steal your identity.

The problem is that if you don't share any information, none of your friends will be able to find you on the site. That defeats the purpose of a social networking site in the first place. On the other hand, if you share too much you may discover that someone else is masquerading under your identity. They might even be destroying your credit rating or attempting to access your e-mail or financial information.

Another danger is that scammers use social networking sites to trick people into downloading malicious software (malware). A common tactic is to use social engineering. Social engineering plays on human nature to get results. For example, you might receive a link from a friend claiming that it leads you to a funny video that you appear in. Following the link brings up a message saying you need to install a video player before you can view the clip. But the video player is actually a virus or Trojan horse program that can harm your computer. Once your computer is infected, the scammer will use your friends list to try and spread the malware even further.

Social networking can be both overwhelming and addictive at the same time. If you join every social network and add hundreds of people as friends, you'll receive updates constantly. It'll become difficult to see any one individual's updates. You'll have a lot of noise to filter out if you want to find something specific. And you may find yourself checking for updates several times throughout the day when you really should be doing something else.

The good news is that the pros for social networking outweigh the cons. And with a few healthy habits, you can avoid or minimise the drawbacks. Just remember to be careful and responsible before you sign up!

■ ■ ■

Reservation

Today, reservation has become a major issue of discussion, dissension, debate and bitterness for a certain section of society in independent India. When India got its freedom from the British yoke in 1947, the framers of the Indian Constitution made these reservations for that section of our society which had been long neglected and disparaged. The purpose was well thought of and in all fairness, in order to enable the downtrodden, improve their status and enter into the mainstream of the country's developmental works.

The basic idea was undoubtedly superb as, it was in all good intent, meant to build up to a certain level those sections of the Indian society which had hitherto been left uncared for. Besides, this was originally to be fixed for only the first fifteen years of independence. This was done so, with the expectation that, one single generation would be turned out in fifteen years and would become capable of joining the others and forging a march ahead. The programme as visualized was rather good, but, what shape it has taken in the last fifty years is for all of us to see, and appreciate. The system has been misused by one and all, just for the betterment of each one's fancy.

The Scheduled Tribes and Scheduled Castes were, originally the only ones who were given this reservation, and that too for fifteen years. It was for this specific period only because, it was expected that, one generation would be helped to rise in this period. However, as we see it today, the policy of reservation has been completely changed in the span of the last fifty years. There has been unlimited extension of the policy for, no one knows how long, it appears as though the policy has come to stay forever and its extension is also as though unlimited, with several more sections joining the bandwagon of the privileged reservationists.

A series of backward classes have now been included to be termed as the OBCs, and the latest category include in the list is of women. There are about than 50% or more of seats reserved everywhere for these classes, and where will all this end up, and, where will the so-called advantaged majority go, if reservations keep rising at this pace nobody knows.

Reservations have come up in educational institutions, in jobs, in state assemblies, in parliament, in every feasible sphere. It will a wonder if this system is really going to help us raise our standards in any sphere at all, or will this become just a tool in the hands of a few, to forward their own interests, as has been upto this juncture. The reservation has been fitted only few families of any weaker section and not the mass in general. The reservation must be restricted to provide education to some state and give employment to one only one. After employment he should not be given any other facility and should be left to raise his family on his shoulders itself. Why a minister's, chief minister's or Deputy Commissioner's son be treated as poor and be given reservation once he is able to raise his family of its own.

Being of a reserved category should give a normal being a feeling of being someone less than others, but, in our present day scenario, it seems we take pride in being one of a reserved category, which shows an absolute lack of self-respect in us Indians. Is reservation something we should hanker for, is it not charity that we want to progress upon? If we are a self respecting community, we should never want any reservation for ourselves. However, we seem to take pride and feel privileged when we are among the reserved class.

Reservation should not be based on caste colour or creed as it is now. The only plausible basis for reservations should be economic status of an individual. Those who cannot afford to be educated in Institutions of repute, and are really interested, should be allowed entry free in order to encourage them to follow their educational pursuits. They should be allowed to grow with the others, and not allowed any lenience in their passing, for, once they have the same educational background as all others, and not allowed any lenience in their passing, why should they have any further advantage over the others. Any lenience to them in the marking schedule etc., destroys the basic standards of our education, and beyond that, the standard of our workers.

Only economic backwardness should be the yardstick for anything like reservation. This policy in its present shape must be scrapped altogether, as, it is leading to more of heart burning than any progress of the backward classes. It is creating more and more confusion on the planning side and more cracks are seen to appear among different sections of society. By this policy what we are in reality achieving is, much too negative a prospect to be of any utility at this point of time. Most of the time we see that, in this process the brilliant children of the upper classes get stranded in their pursuits of education or job hunting because the vacancies are reserved for only the

Scheduled Castes or Scheduled Tribes. This puts in the minds of these good students a hatred for these classes, and this not wrongly so. So, instead of doing away with the class evil, the system is making the demarcation still deeper. It gives a sense of frustration to the upper classes and at the same time, an unwanted boost in the aspirations of the Scheduled Classes. They begin to feel that theirs are the reserved seats, so they do not have to make any effort. In this way, the reservation policy is helping to widen the gap between the two classes instead of bridging it, for which the policy was originally meant. On the work front also, when we put in less capable people just because the job is reserved for them, the work bound to suffer.

Regarding this policy, if at all it has to be maintained indefinitely, it should be reservations only for the economically backward, and not based on any other criteria. Besides, reservations should be only for education and that also, only for those who are economically weak. There should be no reservations for anyone at all in jobs, for, when all have had the same education, they are all equally capable to enter any competition in the open job market and all at par so no reservations are required. For this system, the education has to be spread even to the poorest of the poor and this education of the best quality must be provided to all free of cost to all people of all castes, creeds and then they should all enter the job hunting spree on their merit. Only if merit is the only criteria we can aspire to get the best quality of individuals getting the best.

Once when a person gets what he deserves, he will have no qualms about favouritism etc. It has often been seen that, all the cream of our children coming out of educational institutions are going out of the country. Of course, money they get outside is one aspect for going out, but another important criterion for this is a feeling of frustration among them while in India. This is because the good students do not really get in India what they truly deserve, for, in several places, the obviously less worthy are placed higher than them due to the very reservation policy. This can and is very detrimental in our achievement of quality.

The reservation has therefore become more of a hoax and a vote catching device rather than serving as a booster to the lower sections of society, and help them rise to any worthwhile levels. The policy was very well meaning in its original setting but, as time has passed, the policy has become as if a convenient cash crop for the politicians in the last five decades. This has been done just to serve their own ends and not to serve the backward classes. Like any other policy of India, this has also become a sham and deceit throughout.

In view of the present scenario, it is needed to keep aside the narrow vote bank politics and think truly for the betterment of the under-privileged and honestly pursue policies and programmes for their upliftment.

■ ■ ■

Commonwealth Games

The Commonwealth Games is an international, multi-sport event involving athletes from the Commonwealth of Nations. As well as many Olympic sports, the Games also include some sports that are played mainly in Commonwealth countries, such as lawn bowls, rugby sevens and netball. The Games are overseen by the Commonwealth Games Federation (CGF), which also controls the sporting programme and selects the host cities. The host city is selected from across the Commonwealth, with eighteen cities in seven countries having hosted it.

The event was first held in 1930 under the title of the British Empire Games in Hamilton, Ontario, Canada. The event was renamed as the British Empire and Commonwealth Games in 1954, the British Commonwealth Games in 1970, and gained its current title in 1978. Only six teams have attended every Commonwealth Games: Australia, Canada, England, New Zealand, Scotland and Wales. Australia has been the highest achieving team for eleven games, England for seven and Canada for one.

There are currently 54 members of the Commonwealth of Nations, and 71 teams participate in the Games. The four Home Nations of the United Kingdom – England, Scotland, Wales and Northern Ireland – send separate teams to the Commonwealth Games, and individual teams are also sent from the British Crown dependencies of Guernsey, Jersey and the Isle of Man (unlike at the Olympic Games, where the combined "Great Britain" team represents all four home nations and the Crown dependencies). Many of the British overseas territories also send their own teams. The Australian external territory of Norfolk Island also sends its own team, as do the Cook Islands and Niue, two states in free association with New Zealand. It was reported that Tokelau, another dependency of New Zealand would be sending a team to the 2010 Games in New Delhi, India. In the end, however, they did not.

A sporting competition bringing together the members of the British Empire was first proposed by the Reverend Astley Cooper in 1891 when he wrote an article in *The Times* suggesting a "Pan-Britannic-Pan-Anglican Contest and Festival every four years as a means of increasing the goodwill and good understanding of the British Empire".

In 1911, the Festival of the Empire was held in London to celebrate the coronation of King George V. As part of the festival an Inter-Empire Championships was held in which teams from Australia, Canada, South Africa and the United Kingdom competed in events such as boxing, wrestling, swimming and athletics.

In 1928, Melville Marks Robinson of Canada was asked to organise the first British Empire Games. The first Games were held in 1930 in Hamilton, Ontario, Canada. The name changed to British Empire and Commonwealth Games in 1954, to British Commonwealth Games in 1970 and assumed the current name of the Commonwealth Games in 1978.

At the 1930 games, women competed in the swimming events only. From 1934, women also competed in some athletics events.

The Empire Games flag was donated in 1931 by the British Empire Games Association of Canada. The year and location of subsequent games were added until the 1950 games. The name of the event was changed to the

British Empire and Commonwealth Games and the flag was retired as a result.
- Commonwealth Winter Games
- Commonwealth Youth Games

Traditions
- From 1930 until 1950, the parade of nations was led by a single flagbearer carrying the Union Flag.
- Since 1958, the Queen's Baton Relay has taken place, in which athletes carry a baton from Buckingham Palace to the games opening ceremony. This baton has within it Queen Elizabeth II's message of greeting to the athletes. The baton's final bearer is usually a famous sporting personage of the host nation.
- All other nations march in English alphabetical order, except that the first nation marching in the Parade of Athletes is the host nation of the previous games, and the host nation of the current games marches last. In 2006 countries marched in alphabetical order in geographical regions.
- Three national flags fly from the stadium on the poles that are used for medal ceremonies: Previous host nation, Current host nation, Next host nation.
- The military is more active in the Opening Ceremony than in the Olympic Games. This is to honour the British Military traditions of the Old Empire

Editions
The first edition of the event was the 1930 British Empire Games and eleven nations took part. The quadrennial schedule of the games was interrupted by World War II and the 1942 Games (set to be held in Montreal) and the 1946 Games were abandoned. The games were continued in 1950 and underwent a name change four years later

with the first British Empire and Commonwealth Games in 1954. Over 1000 athletes participated in the 1958 Games as over thirty teams took part for the first time.

The event was briefly known as the British Commonwealth Games for the 1970 and 1974 editions and the 1978 Games, held in Edmonton, Canada, were the first to be held under the title of the "Commonwealth Games". The Edmonton event marked a new high as almost 1500 athletes from 46 countries took part.

Participation at the 1986 Games was affected by a boycott by some African and Caribbean nations in protest to the participation of New Zealand, following the All Blacks Rugby tour of Apartheid era South Africa in 1985, but the Games rebounded and continued to grow thereafter. The 1998 Commonwealth Games in Kuala Lumpur, Malaysia saw the sporting programme grow from 10 to 15 sports as team sports were allowed for the first time. Participation also reached new levels as over 3500 athletes represented 70 teams at the event. At the Games in Melbourne in 2006, over 4000 athletes took part in sporting competitions.

The three nations to have hosted the games the most number of times are Australia (4), Canada (4) and New Zealand (3). Furthermore, five editions have taken place in the countries within the United Kingdom (Scotland 2, England 2 and Wales 1). Two cities have held the games on multiple occasions: Auckland (1950 and 1990), and Edinburgh (1970 and 1986).

The two principal bids for the 2010 Commonwealth Games, officially known as the XIX Commonwealth Games, were from Delhi, India and Hamilton, Ontario, Canada. The Games, were held in Delhi, India, from 3 to 14 October 2010.

It was the first time that the Commonwealth Games were held in India and the second time it was held in Asia after Kuala Lumpur, Malaysia in 1998. The opening and closing ceremonies were held at the Jawaharlal Nehru Stadium. The official mascot of the Games was Shera. A.R. Rahman composed the official song of the Games, 'Jiyo Utho Bado Jeeto'.

A total of 6,081 athletes from 71 Commonwealth nations and dependencies competed in 21 sports and 272 events. It was the largest international multi-sport event to be staged in Delhi and India, eclipsing the Asian Games in 1951 and 1982.

Initially, several concerns and controversies surfaced before the start of the Games. Despite these concerns, all member nations of the Commonwealth of Nations participated in the event, except Fiji, which is suspended from the Commonwealth, and Tokelau, which didn't send a team.

The opening ceremony played a key role in improving the image of the Games. As athletes arrived and competitions started, many earlier critics changed their view. The Australian Sports Minister said that India could now aim for the Olympics, and the President of the International Olympic Committee, Jacques Rogge, said that India had made a good foundation for a future Olympics bid.

As the Games concluded, many observers remarked that they began on an apprehensive note, but were an exceptional experience with a largely positive ending. The final medal tally was led by Australia. The host nation India gave its strongest performance yet to emerge second, while England placed third.

■■■

Black Money

Black money refers to funds earned on the black market, on which income and other taxes have not been paid.

Recently it came into view that according to the data provided by the Swiss bank, India has more black money than rest of the world combined.

India tops the list with almost $1500 Billion black money in Swiss banks, followed by Russia $470 Billion, UK $390 Billion, Ukraine $100 Billion and China with $96 Billion.

In January 2011, the Supreme Court of India asked why the names of those who have stashed money in the Liechtenstein Bank have not been disclosed. The court argued that the government should be more forthcoming in releasing all available information on the money that is believed to be held in illegally in foreign banks.

In August 2010, the government revised the Double Taxation Avoidance Agreement to provide means for investigations of black money in Swiss banks.

This revision, expected to become active by January 2012, will allow the government to make inquiries of Swiss banks in cases where they have specific information about possible black money being stored in Switzerland.

To curb black money, India has signed TIEA with 10 countries – Bahamas, Bermuda, the British Virgin islands, the Isle of Man, the Cayman Island, the British island of Jersey, Monaco, St. Kitts and Nevis, Argentina and the

Marshal Islands – where money is believed to have been stashed away.

It's embarrassing for any country to top the list of black money holders. The money which belongs to the nation and its citizens is stashed in the illegal personal accounts of corrupt politicians, IRS, IPS officers and industrialists. The only hope Indians harbour is a revolution against corruption, which only they have the power to initiate.

Unfortunately, the common man here is so burdened with the responsibilities of daily life that he is caught in the vicious circle of making money to fulfil his own needs.

■■■

Egypt Crisis

The crisis in Egypt over the past few months has reached alarming levels. Tens of thousands of Egyptian people have taken out to the streets and are demanding nothing less than the ouster of its President Hosni Mubarak. There have been massive protests all over the country with many episodes of violence being reported. The hot bed of it all is in Capital Cairo at the Tahrir Square which has witnessed an incredible number of protestors. The army and the people have been at constant loggerheads over the course of the entire week.

Lives are continuing to be lost and scores are being injured on a daily basis. There is a lot of anger in the people which probably is one of the reasons why the protests seem to show no signs of letting down after more than a week. In fact more and more violent incidents are being recorded with each passing day. So much so that, President Hosni Mubarak has finally agreed to step down within six months time, but the opposition and public are unrelenting and are seeking an immediate ouster. Here is a look at some of the main reasons why this situation has come about.

Egypt over the years

Egypt is a large country which is mostly Arab and predominantly Muslim populated. A major part of the country is located North of Africa and part of the country borders with Israel. It other neighbours are Sudan (to the South), Libya (to the West), and Saudi Arabia (across the Gulf of Aqaba to the East. With a population of close to 80 million it is the country with the largest population in the Middle East and also third largest in Africa.

It is currently being ruled by President Hosni Mubarak who has occupied the post for close to thirty years now since the assassination of Anwar Sadat in 1981. The 82-year-old Mubarak has often been accused of being an autocratic dictator and has been known to suppress political parties, banning Islamic oppositions groups, using excessive police force to deal with suspects and other voices of dissent like the media. His government is also guilty of massive corruption and widespread poverty.

Why are the protests happening now?

The trigger came about in December when a street fruit vendor in Tunisia set himself on fire, killing himself to protest government corruption. Huge numbers of people took to the streets to protest against rampant unemployment, excessive policing, inflated food prices and the repressive style of governance. It resulted in the ouster of Tunisia's president of 23 years, Zine El Abidine Ben Ali, after many days of violent protests. The ripple of dissent could be felt across Morocco, Jordan, Yemen, Syria and now Egypt.

Furthermore with Egypt's Presidential elections due in September there was speculation that Mubarak's son Gamal might contest even if Mubarak didn't himself. This did not give the people much to hope for.

What are these protestors seeking?

The protestors are seeking an end to the autocratic form

Egypt Crisis

of governance. The police state rule and the three decade old emergency state law severely restricts political activity and even peaceful demonstrations. Corruption, unemployment and non affordability of food where others reasons that deeply angered the Egyptian people.

Food also over the years has evolved into a political issue in Egypt. It is the world's biggest importer and consumer of wheat. Most of the people are poor and constant inflation of food prices was making daily survival difficult.

Egypt is currently ranked 138th of 167 countries on *The Economist's Democracy Index*, a widely accepted measure of political freedom.

Mubarak's Opposition Leaders

At this point of time all the leaders with good enough clout is still unclear. One of Mubarak's main opposition is the Muslim Brotherhood which he had banned earlier. Another popular rival is the high profile and Nobel Laureate Mohamed ElBaradei who is riding a wave of popularity after being put under house arrest by Mubarak's forces. He is being looked upon as someone who could possibly take over the reigns if Mubarak is ousted.

The issue keeps snowballing with every passing day. While other nations are applying diplomatic pressure to bring a logical solution to this entire problem it remains to be seen how this situation would finally turn out.

To prepare for the overthrow of Mubarak, opposition groups studied the work of Gene Sharp on non-violent revolution and worked with leaders of Otpor!, the student-

Serbian uprising of 2000. Copies of Sharp's list of 198 non-violent 'weapons', translated into Arabic, were circulated in Tahrir Square during its occupation.

After the ousting of Tunisian president Zine El Abidine Ben Ali due to mass protests, many analysts, including former European Commission President Romano Prodi, saw Egypt as the next country where such a revolution might occur.

The *Washington Post* commented, "The Jasmine Revolution [...] should serve as a stark warning to Arab leaders – beginning with Egypt's 83-year-old Hosni Mubarak – that their refusal to allow more economic and political opportunity is dangerous and untenable."

■ ■ ■

Aggression in Human Beings

Aggression is something that all animals have. There are many different levels of aggression and people, as well as other animals, act on their feelings of aggression in many different ways. Aggression comes in many forms including physical violence, sexual abuse, yelling and mental abuse. There are many factors that contribute to the amount of aggressiveness that people have and the ways that they act on them. Males generally have more aggression than women and act out with aggressive behaviours more often. Aggression and anger can be controlled and treated in several different ways. Aggression can not be completely destroyed, as it is a basic animal instinct.

Everyone human on earth has aggression already in his or her biology. Some people have more than others do and some act on theirs more, but everyone has it. Studies have shown that males generally tend to have more aggression than woman. This has been shown through studies done about the link between testosterone and aggressive behaviour. In a study done of 4,462 menz showed that higher testosterone levels showed increases in delinquency in adolescence and substance abuse. It also showed that as children they often had trouble with teachers and later in life had more sexual partners and used hard drugs. The study also revealed that among inmates the ones with higher testosterone levels committed violent crimes, more likely to be rejected for release by the parole board, and had more prison rule violations.

There are two other biological factors that may play a role in the prevalence of aggressive behaviour. One of these is a brain chemical called seratonin. Seratonin sometimes acts as a behavioural inhibitor. People that have a lower level of seratonin often show increased levels of impulsivity and aggressiveness. They are not as self conscious about their behaviours so they act on pure instinct more than others. Two other chemicals in the brain, dopamine and norepinephrine, are also believed to contribute to aggressive behaviour.

Another cause of aggressive behaviour is believed to come in early childhood. If a child is abused or sees abuse occur, they are more likely to be abusive in their adulthood. Not only does it cause the child to become abusive later in life, abuse has an adverse affect on them immediately. They are often very fearful, have nightmares, feel powerless, have poor school performance, are more likely to abuse substances, are sexually promiscuous, have stomach cramps, headaches, sleeping and eating disorders and are frequently ill.

Although there are many different ways that males take out their aggression, one of the most prevalent symptoms of males with aggressive behaviour is domestic violence. This destroys many families and hurts wives, children, and the attacker (usually the husband). Of all assault cases reported, many are spousal abuse and so many all hospital emergency room visits are related to domestic violence. Even with these high percentages, abused women and children need medical attention. This shows that many cases of domestic abuse probably go unreported.

Another way in which males act out on their aggressive thoughts is through rape or sexual assault. Many people may think that these are crimes of sexual passion, but often times they are crimes of intense anger and aggression. The attacker is trying to be in control. Rape doesn't always occur by a stranger in some dark alley. In fact, about seventy per cent of rape and sexual assault victims know their attacker. So many college age girls will be victims of sexual assault.

Another cause of aggression, and one that often leads to sexual assault is alcohol. Many sexual assaults on a college campus involve alcohol or drugs. In fact, maximum of homicide offenders, some of assault offenders, some of sexual offenders, some of marital abuse and child abuse involve alcohol. Alcohol disrupts normal brain functions by weakening brain mechanisms that normally restrain people from acting out impulsive behaviours, including inappropriate aggression. Another reason why alcohol may add to aggressive behaviour is because the person's thoughts are altered. This may lead to them overreacting to a social threat, or they can't correctly assess the consequences that may come from their violent behaviour.

One of the most effective techniques to reducing aggressiveness and violence is through counselling and therapy. There are many different ways that this can be done, from anger management classes, to group therapy, to one on one sessions. Anger management therapy allows the person to learn more about their anger. Most anger management services try to provide a "warm, comfortable, safe and therapeutic environment." This makes it so that the patient does not feel like they are being punished. The idea is for the people to get better, not for them to feel threatened.

First a patient's behaviour and anger must be assessed. Once this is done then a course of action can be picked. The successive appointments will follow along this course and try to discover the roots of the aggression and hopefully turned around. The counselling hoes to change unhealthy anger responses to new, more productive ways of dealing with anger rather than violence. People involved in therapy will find the origin of their anger and what type of anger they have. That is what they like to do to act out their aggression. They will be taught how to manage their anger and how to release it in a safe and supportive environment. Also patients will learn how to reduce high levels of stress, manage anxiety, and reduce depression, all of which are causes of aggression.

One on one counseling is the most effective technique in anger management. It allows each person's individual needs to be addressed, because no two persons' anger and aggression are the same. Group therapy is also effective but does not give the people the individual attention that they need. When in therapy people's aggression can be greatly reduced, but it can never be "cured". It is a basic instinct that we all have, just some people act on it more than others, and this must be controlled. Therapy takes a long time and will help to reduce the outbursts, but the aggression will still always be there.

Aggression is found in every living animal on earth. It is often shown in many different ways. It is a necessary emotion because it helps us to release anger. However there are good and bad ways of releasing aggression. When released in bad ways violence often occurs, whether it is domestic, sexual or homicidal. Both males and females have aggression, but males are more likely to act out on it because of their higher levels of testosterone, a cause for aggression. Other causes include alcohol and video games. Treating aggression can be a hard and long process, usually done by therapy. Aggression adversely affects many people's lives. It causes divorce, incarceration, hospitalization and even death. Aggression can never be fully done away with because all beings are born with it and can act on it from the moment of birth. People just need to learn how to control it.

■ ■ ■

State of India's Current Economy

In the second half of 2008-09, there was a significant slowdown in the growth rate, following the financial crisis that hit the world in 2007. The fiscal year 2009-10, thus, began on a difficult note. There was an apprehension that the slow-down will continue to affect the economy thus making 2009-10 a difficult year.

However, 2009-10 turned out to be a year of reckoning for the policy-makers, who took a calculated risk by providing substantial fiscal expansion to counter the negative fallout of the global slowdown. The downside of the fiscal stimulus was that India's fiscal deficit increased, reaching 6.8 per cent of GDP in 2009-10. A sub-normal monsoon added to the overall uncertainty. Despite of all odds, the economy, at the end of the financial year, posted a remarkable recovery, not only in terms of overall growth figures but, more importantly, in terms of certain fundamentals, which justify optimism for the Indian economy in the medium to long-term.

The real turnaround came in the second quarter of 2009-10 when the economy grew by 7.9 per cent. As per the advance estimates of GDP for 2009-10, released by the Central Statistical Organization (CSO), the economy is expected to grow at 7.2 per cent in 2009-10, with the industrial and the service sectors growing at 8.2 and 8.7 per cent respectively.

This recovery is impressive for at least three reasons. First, it has come about despite a decline of 0.2 per cent in agricultural output, which was the consequence of sub-normal monsoons. Second, it fore-shadows renewed momentum in the manufacturing sector, which had seen continuous decline in the growth rate for almost eight quarters since 2007-08. Indeed, manufacturing growth has more than doubled from 3.2 per cent in 2008-09 to 8.9 per cent in 2009-10. Third, there has been a recovery in the growth rate of gross fixed capital formation, which had declined significantly in 2008-09 as per the revised National Accounts Statistics (NAS). While the growth rates of private and government final consumption expenditure have dipped in private consumption demands, there has been a pick-up in the growth of private investment demands.

There had also been a turnaround in merchandise export growth in November 2009, which had been sustained in December 2009, after a decline in nearly twelve continuous months. The broad-based nature of the recovery created scope for a gradual rollback, in due course, some of the measures undertaken to overcome global slowdown effects on Indian economy, so as to put the economy back on to the growth path of 9 per cent per annum. The emergence of high double-digit food inflation during the second half of the financial year 2009-10 is a major cause of concern.

On a year-on-year basis, wholesale price index (WPI) headline inflation in December 2009 was 7.3 per cent, but for food items (primary and manufactured), with a combined weight of 25.4 per cent in the WPI basket, it was 19.8 per cent. A significant part of this inflation was due to supply-side bottle-necks in some of the essential commodities, precipitated by the delayed and sub-normal southwest monsoons.

Overall GDP Growth

The CSO has effected a revision in the base year from 1999-2000 to 2004-05. It includes changes on account of certain refinements in definitions of some aggregates, widening of coverage, inclusion of long-term survey results and the normal revision in certain data in respect of 2008-09. While there are no major changes in the overall growth rate of GDP at constant 2004-05 prices, except for 2007-08 where it has been revised upward from 9.0 to 9.2 per cent, there are some changes in growth rates at sectoral level and in the level estimates of GDP. The contribution of the agriculture sector to the GDP at factor cost in 2004-05 has declined from 17.4 per cent in the old series to 15.9 per cent in the new series.

There is also an increase in the contribution of real estate, ownership of dwellings and business services from 8.2 per cent to 8.9 per cent.

In the case of level estimates of GDP at current prices, the difference ranges from 3.1 per cent in 2004-05 to 6 per cent in 2008-09. As a result, there are also changes in the expenditure estimates of the GDP. The advance estimate of GDP growth at 7.2 per cent for 2009-10, falls within the range of 7 +/- 0.75 projected nearly a year ago in the Economic Survey 2008-09. With the downside risk to growth due to the delayed and sub-normal monsoons having been contained to a large extent, through the likelihood of a better-than-average rabi agricultural season, the economy responded well to the policy measures undertaken in the wake of the global financial crisis.

While the GDP at factor costs at constant 2004-05 prices, is placed at Rs. 44,53,064 crore, the GDP at market prices, at constant prices, is estimated at Rs. 47,67,142 crore. The corresponding figures at current prices are Rs. 57,91,268 crore and Rs. 61,64,178 crore, respectively. The recovery in GDP growth for 2009-10 is broad based. Seven out of eight sectors/sub-sectors show a growth rate of 6.5 per cent or higher. The exception is agriculture and allied sectors where the growth rate is estimated to be minus 0.2 per cent over 2008-09. Sectors, including mining and quarrying, manufacturing; and electricity, gas and water supply have significantly improved their growth rates at over 8 per cent in comparison with 2008-09.

The construction sector and trade, hotels, transport and communication have also improved their growth rates over the preceding year, though to a lesser extent.

However, the growth rate of community, social and personal services has declined significantly, though it continues to be around its pre-global crisis medium-term trend growth rate.

Financing, insurance, real estate and business services have retained their growth momentum at around 10 per cent in 2009-10.

In terms of sectoral shares, the share of agriculture and allied sectors in GDP at factor cost has declined gradually from 18.9 per cent in 2004-05 to 14.6 per cent in 2009-10. During the same period, the share of industry has remained the same at about 28 per cent, while that of services has gone up from 53.2 per cent in 2004-05 to 57.2 per cent in 2009-10.

Per capita Growth

The growth rates in per capita income and consumption, which are gross measures of welfare in general, have declined since 2008. This is a reflection of the slowdown in the overall GDP growth.

While the growth in per capita income, measured in terms of GDP at constant market prices, has declined from a high of 8.1 per cent in 2007-08 to 3.7 per cent in 2008-09 and then recovered to 5.3 per cent in 2009-10, per capita consumption growth as captured in the private final consumption expenditure (PFCE) shows a declining trend since 2007-08 with its growth rate in 2009-10 falling to one-third of that in 2007-08.

The average growth in per capita consumption over the period 2005-06 to 2009-10 was slower at 6.08 per cent than that in per capita income at 6.52 per cent. These year to year differences in growth rates can be explained by the rising savings rate and also the rise in tax collections that have been observed in some of these years.

Agriculture

Total foodgrains production in 2008-09 was estimated at 233.88 million tonnes as against 230.78 million tonnes in 2007-08 and 217.28 million tonnes in 2006-07. In the agricultural season 2009-10, the impact of the delayed and sub-normal monsoon is reflected in the production and acreage data for kharif crops. As per the first advance estimates, covering only the kharif crop, production of foodgrains is estimated at 98.83 million tonnes in 2009-10, as against the fourth advance estimates of 117.70 million tonnes for the kharif crop in 2008-09 and a target of 125.15 million tonnes for 2009-10.

Overall production of kharif cereals in 2009-10 has shown a decline of 18.51 million tonnes over 2008-09.

In terms of acreage, the kharif 2009-10 season saw a

State of India's Current Economy

decline of nearly 6.5 per cent or 46.18 lakh ha in the area covered under foodgrains. Almost the entire decline in this acreage was confined to the kharif rice crop. Some of this decline in acreage may have been made up by the increased acreage in the rabi season.

Road Ahead

There are some deep changes that have taken place in India, which suggest that the economy's fundamentals are strong. First, the rates of savings and investment have reached levels that even ten years ago would have been dismissed as a pipedream for India. On this important dimension, India is now completely a part of the world's fast growing economies.

In 2008-09 gross domestic savings as a percentage of GDP were 32.5 per cent and gross domestic capital formation 34.9 per cent. These figures, which are a little lower than what had been achieved before the fiscal stimulus was put into place, fall comfortably within the range of figures one traditionally associated with the East Asian economies. Since these indicators are some of the strongest correlates of growth and do not fluctuate wildly, they speak very well for India's medium-term growth prospects. It also has to be kept in mind that as the demographic dividend begins to pay off in India, with the working age-group population rising disproportionately over the next two decades, the savings rate is likely to rise further. Second, the arrival of India's corporations in the global market place, and informal indicators of the sophisticated corporate culture that many of these companies exhibit, lends to the optimistic prognosis for the economy in the medium to long-run. In the medium-term it is reasonable to expect that the economy will go back to the robust growth path of around 9 per cent that it was on before the global crisis slowed it down in 2008. To begin with, there has been a revival in investment and private consumption demand, though the recovery is yet to attain the pre-2008 momentum. Second, Indian exports have recorded impressive growth in November and December 2009 and early indications of the January 2010 data on exports are also encouraging.

Hence, going by simple calculations based on the above-mentioned variables, coupled with the fact that agriculture did have a set-back in 2009 and is only gradually getting back to the projected path, a reasonable forecast for the year 2010-11 is that the economy will improve its GDP growth by around 1 percentage point from that witnessed in 2009-10. Thus, allowing for factors beyond the reach of domestic policy-makers, such as the performance of the monsoon and rate of recovery of the global economy, the Indian GDP can be expected to grow around 8.5, with a full recovery breaching the 9 per cent mark in 2011-12.

■■■